HEALING

Disquiet

AN INTEGRATIVE MODEL FOR RELATIONAL THERAPY

SAM BERG, DMIN

Living Water Press

Published by:
Living Water Press
Box 429, Mossbank, Saskatchewan, Canada, S0H 3G0

The scripture quotations in this book are
used with permission, specifically:
NIV – the Holy Bible, New International Version
Copyright © 1973, 1978, 1984, 2011 by Biblica, Inc. (All rights reserved)
ESV – the Holy Bible, English Standard Version
Copyright © 2001 by Crossway. (All rights reserved)

ISBN: 978-1990-863-59-2 (eBook)
ISBN: 978-1990-863-58-5 (Hardcover)
ISBN: 978-1990-863-57-8 (Paperback)

To contact the author:
https://linktr.ee/Healing.Disquiet

Dedication

To Erika

To our children: Garry and Ida-Marie

To our grandchildren: Seleana, Eva, Ben, Brianna, Sophie, and Mila

And to those in my life who have been my family crucible:
Parents Jake and Enga Berg, siblings Paul, Liz, Steve and Joanne,
their partners, and all the nieces and nephews they have produced
now going on to the next generation.

Contents

Introduction 1

Chapter 1 - Introduction to An Integrated Model 7
    A. An Integrative Model 10
    B. The Politics of Words 12
    C. The Bible-Psychology Debate 19
    D. Conclusion 20

Chapter 2 - Issues and Possibilities About Integration of
Models and Disciplines of Theology and Psychology 22

Chapter 3 - Biblical Anthropology: A Biblical
Understanding of Human Persons 34
    A. The Importance of Biblical Anthropology 36
    B. Significant Biblical Texts 37
    C. Embodiment 40
    D. Sexuality 41
    E. Human Beings as Communal Beings 44
    F. Human Beings as Originally Good 53

Chapter 4 - The Systemic and Relational Approach to
Psychotherapy: The Systemic Theory of Murray Bowen 55
    A. Basic Systemic Concepts That Shaped Family Therapy ... 56
    B. History of the Early Family Therapy Movement 61
    C. Early Pioneers of the Family Therapy Movement 66
    D. Bowenian Family Therapy 77

Chapter 5 - The Personal Aspect of Understanding Humans 99

    A. The Personal Capacity...100

    B. Rational Capacity..102

    C. Volitional Capacity 108

    D. Emotional Capacity 113

    E. A 5th Capacity - Social Capacity 126

Chapter 6 - Narrative Therapy: Practices for Effective

Relational Counselling.. 129

    A. Social Constructionism.......................................130

    B. Narrative Therapy Practices...............................135

Conclusion 157

References 161

Acknowledgements... 175

About the Author 179

Introduction

What could I ask to bring forth generativity within this relational disquiet? was written on the barrel of the free pen in my hand. I was sitting at a conference celebrating the 50th anniversary of the Calgary Family Therapy Centre and a half a century of contributions to the field of family therapy by family therapist Karl Tomm. Many registrants at the conference had contributed to a lively pre-conference email exchange on the subject before arriving to the event held in August of 2023 where the topic was being discussed further.

One respondent to the online conversation had said that she had only heard the word "disquiet" many years ago in church. "Why art thou cast down, O my soul? And why art thou **disquieted** in me? Hope thou in God: For I shall yet praise him for the help of his countenance" (Psalm 42:5, KJV).

Relational disquiet is a vivid description of the kinds of things that affect us in our relationships. It connotes not only the initial disruption in a relationship but also the ongoing experience of life following the disruption. This book presents an approach to understanding and healing relational disquiet. I hope that it will provide useful ideas for practitioners, pastors, and others involved in the ministry of healing relational disquiet.

My own journey into this work began like this:

I served for 18 years as the pastor of a church in suburban Ottawa, Ontario. Late one evening, early in our time at this church, after I had gone to bed, the phone rang. It was someone who attended our church. He said, "I just hit my wife. Could you come over?" I could and I did. I realized that they hadn't covered this in my seminary training. Another Sunday, a new family attended our church. There were six people: a man, a woman and four children. This represented a 16% growth of our little congregation. I learned from the couple that they were married—but not to each other. She had asked her alcoholic husband to leave the house. The man had met this woman at a community function, and they had started a relationship. He left his family of seven and moved in with her and her two children. Now they were looking for a church. My seminary training had *definitely* not covered this.

I decided I needed to know more, so I found a doctoral program in ministry to marriage and family at Palmer Seminary in Philadelphia where I was introduced to the ideas of marriage and family systems, and of the relational contexts in which people live. A new world of possibilities opened up for me, this training, enhancing both my ministry in my local church as well as in the larger community in which we lived.

Eleven years after receiving my Doctor of Ministry degree, I was invited to join the faculty of Briercrest College and Seminary as the faculty member in charge of the counselling program.

The ideas presented here are the product of dialogues with colleagues, supervisors and mentors, the students that I have had the privilege of teaching and supervising—and the many clients I have had the privilege of conversing over all of those years. I have continued to be fascinated by the discoveries and developments in the field of marriage and family and it is my hope that the reader will discover that same fascination.

The book consists of six chapters that describe what I called "Foundations of Marriage and Family Therapy," the introductory course that I taught to counselling students at Briercrest College and Seminary. "Foundations" sounds a bit pretentious but describes some of the basic ideas that I believe are useful for students to become practitioners. The first chapter is an introduction to points of discussion about the work: What should we call ourselves? How do we know what we know? Why does this all matter? And how do we do this? These are the questions that we seek to answer in this book provide a starting point for those who are called to the practice, profession and ministry of counselling and psychotherapy.

The second chapter is a more detailed, yet very brief review of the integration of ideas from the fields of theology and human behaviour. It seeks to introduce the reader to the area and provide a tentative conclusion about how Christian therapists can be congruent in their faith and provide therapy informed by the best scientific findings of the field of psychotherapy and family therapy. It is informed by the growing body of literature that comes under the broad heading of integration of theology and theory.

The third chapter provides a discussion of biblical anthropology and seeks to answer the question of what makes human beings human.

What are the things we need to understand about ourselves and our relationships that will provide a vision of what humans might become? The chapter includes a discussion of the biblical concept of the *imago Dei* with a discussion of both the individualistic and the communal aspects of that concept. One important foundational idea for relational therapy is that we are created in the image of God communally as well as individually. In western individualistic cultures, the concept of *imago Dei* is usually seen as descriptive of each person; each of us bears the image of God. The communal aspect, that the whole human race together bears the image of God, is often overlooked.

The fourth chapter, on the basis of the communal realities of human existence, presents the basic ideas of systemic theory, and especially as described in the work of family therapy pioneer Murray Bowen. The key idea here is the vision of self-differentiation, the ability of mature people to have the ability to live interdependently. The biblical integrative piece here is the vision of maturity as it is described in Ephesians 4. In contrast to that vision of maturity, I describe each of the other interlocking systemic concepts, triangles, nuclear family emotional processes, family projection processes, multigenerational transmission processes, sibling positions, emotional cutoffs and emotional processes in society. The driving force behind all of these obstacles to growth towards self-differentiation is anxiety, which shows up in each of these other concepts.

The fifth chapter describes human functioning from an individualistic perspective. Inspired by the work of Larry Crabb (2013), it considers the four capacities of human functioning: the personal, the cognitive, the volitional, and the emotional. It is still important for counsellors to have a concept of what has often been called psychodynamic theory.

Essentially, while we are members of families and communities, we are also in(ter)dependent agents. We think and act and feel, not necessarily in that order. In our work with our clients, these subjects of thoughts, emotions, actions, and intentions will always be part of the conversation.

The sixth chapter introduces the practices of narrative therapy as a way of congruently working with people. These practices provide the student with a way of learning to be present in a counselling relationship. The previous chapters provide the "what" of therapy and provide the possibility of educated intuition. They provide several important ideas about what to think about while participating in a counselling conversation, but they do not provide a naturally derived method, technique, or system of counselling practices. This, the sixth chapter seeks to do so by providing the "how" of therapy. Narrative therapy practices such as externalizing, double listening, re-authoring, re-membering, have grown out of reflection on the ways of participating in conversation, the counsellor's role, and the stance towards the counsellee. It attends to the detailed assumptions, presuppositions, intentions, and wordings of the questions that become an essential skill of the counsellor (Tomm, 1987, 1988). Essentially, the stance is one of profound respect for the personhood, relational and social context of the client, and an equally profound humility with regard to one's own expertise. We seek to learn to be decentred—in that the client's story and not the therapist's assessment and techniques is the focus of the conversation—and yet influential in recognizing the effects of the therapist's questions in directing the conversation.

Taken together, the six chapters provide a starting point for people who are called to the privilege of becoming counsellors, and for those who are curious about what counselling is about.

CHAPTER 1

Introduction to An Integrated Model

Suppose you are a counsellor, and you have a client who comes in and says, "I'm depressed!" What is the first question you might ask?

Then, ask yourself, where did your question come from? Did it come from your own experience of having depression? Did it come from your friendship with someone you know who has suffered from depression? From an article or a book you recently read about depression? Our questions always come from somewhere.

The approach to counselling that this book presents contains a bias towards asking good questions; questions that require thought and reflection and evaluation. Our questions come from our experiences and our training, from the relationships we have, and from the communities in which we live and work. It's vital that we understand these sources of our therapeutic questions, understand the presuppositions and assumptions that lie behind them, and appreciate the richness they provide for us in our counselling work.

The concept of reflexive questioning is an old one. Consider these two profound questions from the first chapters of the bible. Genesis 3 contains the account of the "Fall" of humanity, where sin and shame entered into human experience. The man and woman have the horrible realization that they are naked, and when they hear the Lord God walking in the garden, they go into hiding. God then asks the question, "Where are you?" I have often wondered about the tone of voice He might have used. Some imagine a harsh, judgmental tone. I imagine a sympathetic, gracious one—His question inviting them to reflect on where they were, what has happened, and what they had done.

This kind of question is called a *reflexive question*. God would have known where they were, after all! The question invited them to think about where they were.

The next chapter, Genesis 4, contains the account of the murder of Abel by his brother Cain. The Lord God asks, "Where is your brother?" Cain's defensiveness comes out in the now famous counter-question, "Am I my brother's keeper?" Nevertheless, the question stands, and Cain is invited to reflect on his actions and his defensiveness.

These are two examples of what Calgary-based psychiatrist Karl Tomm (1987a, b, 1988) describes as reflexive questions, questions that invite the questioned person to reflect on their situation, and to evoke through the questions the possibilities of life, and their longings for their lives. Karl Tomm studied and published extensively on the use of questions in therapy. This book will explore his taxonomy about questions in a more detailed way in further chapters.

Did you notice the nearly hypnotic effect of my question in the first paragraph: "What's the first question you might ask?" Note how this question directed your attention towards questions and away from a number of other possible practices.

Every question is influential. Every question is directive. Every question is an intrusion. There is no such thing as non-directive counselling. Our questions are our best tools.

This book will explore one set of sources of our questions, namely, a set of counselling theories and practices, the narrative backdrop of these theories and practices, and an understanding of who people are, how problems develop, and how people change (Haley, 1996).

We will consider the following set of three theoretical sources for questioning:

1. A biblical anthropology that develops an understanding of the image of God which the bible presents as the fundamental starting point.
2. Family systems theory which brings to our work an understanding of who we are as people in relationships, within and beyond families.
3. Psychodynamic ideas which incorporate into this theoretical system the inner workings of our beings—such as thoughts, emotions, intentions, and actions.

These theoretical bases can them be applied to two particular approaches to counselling practice:

1. Narrative therapy, an approach to counselling that attends to the language of the client and our attention to the interpretive lens we bring to the conversation (a lens es that is are informed

by our training and shaped by our understanding of our particular location in the counselling relationship).

2. Emotionally focused therapy, which was originally developed as a way of working with couples but has since been expanded to include individuals and families.

These bases and approaches form the framework for an integrated counselling model involving eclecticism and selective borrowing.

A. An Integrative Model

An integrated model is thought of as a wholistically, logically, and conceptually coherent approach to understanding and practicing the science and art of psychotherapy. In their 12th edition of *Family Therapy: Concepts and Methods,* Nichols and Davis contrast integration with *eclecticism,* which they describe as "a little bit of this and a little bit of that," a collection of techniques without a conceptual focus. They also contrast integration with *selective borrowing,* namely, the incorporation of techniques from other approaches into your preferred way of counselling that are also congruent with your approach. There are many useful techniques developed by many theoretical *researchers,* many of which may find their way into the practitioner's approach to the work, but an *integrated* approach would adopt those practices that are congruent with the overall philosophy of who people are, what causes problems, and how people change.

Instead of eclecticism or selective borrowing, the model presented in this book is a third approach to integration, one that is wholistically, logically and conceptually coherent in the way it brings together and integrates theory and practice, theology and application, while providing a clear map for the practitioner.

In an earlier edition of the text *Family Therapy: Concepts and Methods*, the authors presented a metaframeworks model (Nichols & Schwarz, *Family Therapy: Concepts and Methods*, 7th ed, pp.354ff) that included the following six core domains. Each of these needs to be included in an integrated model:

- Intra-psychic process
- Family organization
- Sequences of family interaction
- Development
- Culture
- Gender

As a more recent example of integration, in the 12th edition of the text *Family Therapy: Concepts and Methods* (2021), the authors describe the *narrative solutions* approach as an integration of *narrative therapy* and *solution-focused brief therapy*. While this integration of these two so-called post-modern approaches to therapy is eloquent, I believe that the clinician needs an educated awareness of each of the six domains listed above from the earlier edition of the text.

The model presented in this book is an integrative model in that it includes these core domains with the addition of a theological foundation. This model makes explicit, from the biblical point of view, what is implicit in it; a notion of what the human being is, and what it means to live well. There is a vision of optimal human functioning that informs all approaches to counselling. Ours is given in the bible. (This will be discussed later in the book in the chapter on the *imago Dei*.)

A simpler way of describing this kind of integration is given by Wolfram Soldan (2018) in his article, *What I Need for Orientation,*

Soldan states that we need two things to do effective therapy. First, we need detective knowledge which we derive from our models and modalities. These form the conceptual grid through which we assess and formulate our responses. Secondly, we need familiarity knowledge which comes from the relationship that we have established with the client.

Thus, an integrative model is one that hangs together conceptually and provides a reliable map for guiding the counsellor through a counselling session.

B. The Politics of Words

In this first chapter, it is useful to examine the language used to describe counselling, and the words and names counsellors give to describe who they are and what they do. This is called the politics of words. Consider the following six labels:

1. Pastoral Counselling

Perhaps the most innocuous term in the field is *pastoral counselling*. It is defined more by who does it than what is done in counselling. David Augsburger in his *Pastoral Counseling Across Cultures* defines it at counselling that is "done by a pastor with counseling skills, within the traditions, beliefs, and resources of the faith community that supports them" (1986, p.15).

2. Christian Counselling

This term is associated with Gary Collins and earlier, with Clyde and Bruce Narramore. Both Narramores, Clyde the uncle and his nephew Bruce, were active in the 1960s and 1970s and have written extensively in the area of Christian counselling. Their writings are still accessible through various outlets. Collins in his *Christian Counseling: A Comprehensive Guide,* gives a two-part definition of Christian counselling: it is help with problems of living, and disciple-making. He thus splits these two functions as if they are two separate issues.

> "(C)ounseling seeks to stimulate personality growth and development; to help individuals cope with the problems of life, inner conflict and with crippling emotions; to provide encouragement and guidance for those who are facing losses or disappointments; and to assist persons whose life patterns are self-defeating and causing unhappiness. In addition, the Christian counselor seeks to bring people into a personal relationship with Jesus Christ and has the ultimate goal of helping others to become first disciples of Christ and then disciplers of others" (1980, p14).

Many Christians in the counselling professions have recognized that this term may be a barrier for potential clients. The agency with which I am associated has changed its public stance in this regard. It presents itself as "faith-based."

3. Biblical Counselling

This term is perhaps most famously associated with Jay Adams whose popular book *Competent to Counsel* made an impression among all those who sought to remain faithful to the scriptures as they practiced counselling and psychotherapy. In part, Adams is reacting to the increasing influence that popular psychology arising out of the humanist and existentialist influences of the mid-last century was having on Christian counsellors.

Adams, writing out of his experience as an intern with well-known psychologist, O. Hobart Mowrer (d. 1982), decided that the bible itself contained far more resources for the work of counselling than Christian counsellors were using. Thus, his was a call to a renewed return to the bible as a foundational resource.

Another important contributor to the biblical counselling movement was Larry Crabb. One of his earliest works is *Effective Biblical Counseling* (1977) in which he presents his case for what he calls *biblical counselling*. In a later work, *Understanding People* (1987), he fleshes out his approach to biblical counselling. My undergraduate degree in psychology, however, conditioned me to detect the psychology in his work—an individualistic, psychodynamic description of who people are in their four capacities: the personal, the rational, the volitional, and the emotional. Crabb claimed to "spoil the Egyptians" in his adoption of psychological ideas and practices. Just as the Israelites "spoiled the Egyptians" (Exodus 3:2) by taking their best gifts on their way out of Egypt, Crabb suggests that Christian counsellors should use the best that the psychological sciences have to offer. Thus, he is much more open to whatever might be useful in psychology while seeking to remain solidly in the biblical counselling world.

One can hear some of the critique of "Christian counselling" implied in the term "biblical counselling," in an attempt to remain faithful to the biblical resources we have been given. This debate has continued apace in the decades since it began. In a 2021 issue of the *Journal of Psychology and Theology* (JPT, 2021, 49, 3), a series of articles discussed the sufficiency of scripture in the practice of counselling.

I, however, was left with the impression that most of the authors were attempting a defence of their faithfulness to the bible without recognizing the pervasive presence of psychological practices in our work and, indeed, in our lives generally.

Psychology, in its briefest definition, is the study of human behaviour. The best biblical counsellors, who believe they are practicing with the utmost faithfulness to the scriptures, are nevertheless observing how their clients are responding to their counsel. What changes are happening as a result of their counsel? Immediately as such a question arises, such counsellors have entered the field of psychology. The real question is not, can Christian counsellors use psychology, but which type of psychology are they using, and how are they using it?

According to the *JPT* articles referred to above, those who do recognize the usefulness of some psychological ideas, strongly emphasize the need to use scripture as a "lens," so that it serves as the baseline and benchmark as to what is allowable and what needs to be disregarded from the field of psychology. While this can be a useful stance, I think that a more common practice, recognized or not, is that we who love the scriptures and love counselling are engaged in a dialogue between the bible and psychology, in which psychological ideas sometimes give insight into scriptures. The bible is not only the sieve that weeds out erroneous ideas, it becomes a partner in the dialogue that we are each engaged in

4. Psychotherapy

Although the term *Psychotherapy* is a culturally popular term, in the past it has often been regarded suspiciously in some parts of the evangelical community. However, over time, just as the two words *counselling* and *psychotherapy* have become more synonymous in popular usage, so too has the acceptability of the term *psychotherapy,* as demonstrated by the adoption of the term in the name of the Professional Association for Christian Counselling and Psychotherapy.

Furthermore, there is biblical reference for acceptability of the term; the word comes from two Greek words, both of which appear in the bible: *psyche* meaning soul or mind, and *therapeuo* meaning to heal. Thus, the word gives the sense of "soul healing."

There has been a tradition of differentiating between "psychotherapy" and "counselling." At the 2009 National Symposium on Inter-Provincial / Territorial Mobility within the Counselling Profession (sponsored by what was then the Canadian Counselling Association), these two traditional definitions were presented:

> Psychotherapy: remedial – a long-term intervention to deal with complex intrapsychic problems

> Counselling: developmental – to enhance psychological wellness by addressing personal growth and developmental issues

This distinction is no longer observed, and the two words have become approximately synonymous in common usage, as indicated in the two examples above.

5. Seelsorge

This is a German word (pronounced as zale-zorgeh) that signifies *soul care* and *soul cure.* The Latin "cura" signifies both care and cure, the original work of Christian "shepherds" as envisioned in 1 Peter 5:1-4. As the etymology of this word is *shepherd, cura* is specifically intended as a function of Christian pastors! Stanley Hauerwas (2022), in his article *Being with the wounded: Pastoral care within the life of the church,* makes a strong case for differentiating *pastoral* care from the work of counsellors more generally. His critique is that pastors have come to be seen as the professional carers, whereas he pleads for a view in which everyone in the church, and everything the church does, is a fulfillment of its obligation for pastoral care.

In the first chapter of his book, *Psychotherapy and the Spiritual Quest,* David Benner (1988) writes that "modern psychology has turned the attention of helpers from the care of souls to the cure of minds." In a later work, *Care of Souls: Revisioning Christian Nurture and Counsel,* he cites William Clebsch and Charles Jaekle who have "suggested that Christian soul care has involved four elements … healing, sustaining, reconciling, and guiding." This is a fulsome description of the work of the church as envisioned by Hauerwas and goes beyond what most clinicians actually get to do. But it's important that clinicians understand their somewhat proscribed place in the larger ministry of the church. I believe that it is vital for Jesus-followers who are being led into the exciting field of counselling to have a healthy understanding of their particular place and role in the overall ministry of the church and its mandate.

A (very) brief history of the care of souls: We conclude this segment on *seelsorge* with a very brief discussion of the beginning of soul-care in the Christian era. The New Testament has several letters written by various authors relating to the care and guidance of the people who make up the fledgling church. A significant passage is 1 Peter 5:1-3:

> So, I exhort the elders among you, as a fellow elder … shepherd
> the flock of God that is among you, exercising oversight, not

under compulsion, but willingly, as God would have you; not for shameful gain, but eagerly; not domineering over those in your charge, but being examples to the flock.

These verses describe not only the responsibilities of the caregiver, but even more importantly speaks to the motive of that person. Thus, it refers, as we will see later, in the discussions we use today, about both the *skills* of the therapist and also the *person* of the therapist.

This issue is described much more fully a few centuries later by Gregory the Great. Born in 540 CE, he wrote a book called *Pastoral Care*. He saw soul care as an art that exceeded all others in the demands it makes on the caring person. Such a person had four requirements:

1. Spiritual wisdom – through a lifetime of scripture study and the application of this learning to one's life. (Mere cognitive understanding isn't enough!)
2. Self-knowledge – when we try to help others without truly knowing ourselves and our capacity for self-deception, we are most likely to hurt both ourselves and those we are trying to help. Psychotherapists have come to call this the danger of countertransference. A more wholistic and less pathological term for this is the requirement of counsellors to be aware of their own experience as they are engaging in the counselling conversation. We use the term "person-of-the-counsellor" for this.
3. Attention to one's purpose and focus, and the need to balance self-care with care of the other.
4. Recognition of the issue of power and authority in the caring relationship, and the temptation to look down on those for whom we care.

I think it is vital for counsellors to understand the long tradition within which we stand as we do this work.

6. Marriage and Family Therapy

The final term we consider in this section is *marriage and family therapy* (MFT). The term is open to easy misunderstanding as it suggests the clientele which it serves. MFTs often are at pains to explain that we do not just meet with couples and families, but very often with individuals with all sorts of "presenting problems." The key marker of MFT is the theoretical foundation in systems theory. The key is the effort to see the problems which bring people to therapy as having a relational context. The immediate context is the family of origin, but that family also exists in a social and cultural context. Thus, counselling conversations include such details.

There have been recent efforts to change the name to make it more inclusive. Thus, couples and family therapy, relational therapy, and other titles have been proposed in the hopes of describing more accurately what MFTs do. So far, most suggestions have still required a sentence to explain them! Our individualistic culture and the language that goes with it makes it difficult to describe relational terms briefly.

C. The Bible–Psychology Debate

To close this chapter, consider again the ongoing debate about the most faithful and effective way of thinking about the ways counsellors should use the bible and psychology. The debate is illustrated most vividly by the book, *Psychology and Christianity: Four Views*, published in 2000. Ten years later, somewhat entertainingly, the book was republished with the title *Psychology and Christianity: Five Views.*

The debate can be seen along a spectrum from seeing psychology as dangerous and only the bible as being necessary, to the other end in which psychology is necessary and the bible can be useful. The biblical counselling movement champions the viewpoint that psychology is unnecessary, indeed harmful. Proponents of this view include David Powlinson and Jay Adams. Powlinson's work, *The Biblical Counseling Movement: History and Context,* is a reasonably comprehensive description particularly of the influence of Jay Adams' work. Another author who holds this view is Larry Crabb. However, in his book *Understanding People* (1987, updated in 2013), he allows that there may be some aspects of the findings of psychology that might be useful while warning that it may also be misleading. In my opinion, he has written a very useful psychology text infused with theological ideas about who we are, what problems are, and how people change.

At the other end of the spectrum are those Christian counsellors who find an understanding of psychology essential to their work. Examples of this include Howard Clinebell's *Basic Types of Pastoral Care and Counseling,* originally published in 1966, with a revised edition in 2011. Edging away from this extreme is McMinn and Campbell's *Integrative Psychotherapy: Toward a Comprehensive Christian Approach* (2017).

Conclusion

During my studies towards my undergraduate degree in psychology, I learned that psychology is the study of human behaviour, because behaviour is more observable than feelings or thoughts. Of course, we are all thinkers and feelers too. We act and think about our actions and reflect on the feelings our actions produce. We then recognize that our emotional reactions lead to other actions.

Psychology is part of everyday life for us all. Pastors who prepare sermons include illustrations because that will hold the hearers' attention; they are seeking to influence behaviour. Churches and counselling centres chose colour schemes that will be conducive to their work; they are seeking to influence the effectiveness of their counselling. This is applied psychology. Everyone who is involved in the work and ministry of counselling is seeking to be influential. The use of questions, as discussed at the beginning of this chapter, is another example of seeking to be influential. Thus, all are involved in using some application of what is known about influencing people, therefore, we all use psychology.

It's not that we should never "trust" psychology, as Bulkley (1993) has stated, but that we understand it well enough to know what is helpful and what is not.

In summary, this chapter has sought to provide a basic introduction to the field of counselling from a Christian perspective, primarily by introducing the reader to some of the debate among Christians who have engaged in the vital ministry of counselling. This has included a discussion of the various terms that have been used by practitioners in this work, and finally a plea for a basic recognition that both theology and psychology are pervasive in human experience, and that a thorough understanding of both fields will provide a strong foundation for people engaged in this work.

CHAPTER 2

Issues and Possibilities About Integration of Models and Disciplines of Theology and Psychology

Integration in the field of counselling is the process of combining theories and ideas from several sources to produce a coherent whole. The uniting theme brings the ideas from various sources into a logical and applicable theory that answers the questions about who people are, what problems are, and how people change. In counselling, the ideas will include philosophical and, in the case of Christians, theological ideas, along with various approaches to the counselling process. At its heart, integration is the process and result of a thematically consistent and principled description of an approach to counselling. The emphasis is on a *singular* approach.

This chapter first distinguishes integration from several things that often pass for integration and then concludes with a brief overview of the model which will be developed more fully in the chapters following.

With the plethora of approaches to counselling available today, it has become fashionable to call oneself an *eclectic*. The danger of an eclectic approach is that the counsellor may not have thought through the theoretical and philosophical assumptions of the practices used, may not discriminate between effective and ineffective methods, and may not be able to justify to themselves or anyone else why they chose a particular practice at a particular therapeutic moment.

In the 6th edition of their book, *Family Therapy: Concepts and Methods*, Nichols and Schwartz provide a very helpful distinction here. They distinguish between *eclecticism*, "an approach that draws from a variety of models and methods," *selective borrowing*, "in which relative purists use a few practices from other approaches," and *specially designed integrative models* that seek to develop a coherent new model based on the ideas and assumptions of earlier models. They further distinguish between three kinds of integrative models, the *theoretical* which draws on a number of influences, the *pragmatic* which combines elements of two complementary approaches, and models developed for specific clinical problems.

It is hoped that the model presented in this book will be thoroughly integrated in that it draws on a theological and philosophical basis, an intrapersonal and interpersonal understanding of human functioning, and includes a congruent description of counselling practices that describe how counsellors might conduct themselves in their work. If one adopts the three distinctions that Nichols and Schwartz have described, this model will thus be a theoretical, integrative model.

It is also hoped that this will be an integrated model in another equally, if not more important, sense. In addition to an integration of the several models drawn from the field of psychotherapy, this model aims to provide an integration based on a particular world view, one that is drawn from a biblically-faithful, Judeo-Christian tradition.

Award-winning author and professor of counselling, Kirk E. Farnsworth describes a "whole-hearted integration" of this sort. In four short chapters in his book, *Wholehearted Integration: Harmonizing Psychology and Christianity through Word and Deed*, he describes a phenomenological psychology and an experiential theology, brought together in an embodied integration. He contrasts "embodied integration" with a "critical integration" which he describes as the application of the "foundational components" (p.79) to the tenets of psychology with the intent to "ferret out" (p.78) the "influence of non-Christian assumptions that steer research in non-Christian directions. Further, this kind of critical integration provides guidelines for discerning which research findings God wants us to regard as true" (p.78). Thus, Farnsworth is critical of the kind of integration that begins with the assumptions that all psychology is dangerous. Psychology is *ubiquitous*. All of us are interested in what motivates us as humans, how our relationships work and how we grow. Granted, many unhelpful things, some dangerous things, and even some downright absurd things have been said by psychologists. But we all play in the same soup. So, an examination of the ingredients in the soup is necessary!

In place of critical integration, Farnsworth presents a phenomenological psychology which he describes as an approach to understanding human existence and behaviour from within, using the psychologist-scientist's own experience as a human being as part of the investigation—the subject and the object, the observed and the observer. This approach recognizes the impossibility of pure objectivity, at least when it comes to humans. We are too much a part of what we are observing to have any hope of pure objectivity.

This contrasts with a more modernistic approach to the science of psychology which seeks an understanding through observation from outside, as if it's possible for humans to get a bird's (or God's) eye view of human behaviour. This approach limits itself primarily to the observation and counting of human behaviours, defining psychology as simply the study of human behaviour, often leaving aside the whole phenomenon of meaning-making that is such a large part of being human.

B.F. Skinner (1938), famed behavioural psychologist, stated this most starkly in his book, *Walden Two*. "By behaviour, then, I mean simply the movement of an organism or of its parts in a frame of reference provided by the organism itself or by various external objects or fields of force" (p.6). He goes on to describe the need for a special jargon for this science, "In English ... we say that an organism *sees* or *feels* objects, *hears* sounds, *tastes* substances, *smells* odors, and *likes* or *dislikes* them; it *wants, seeks* and *finds;* it *has a purpose, tries* and *succeeds* or *fails;* it *learns* and *remembers* or *forgets;* it is *frightened, angry, happy* or *depressed; asleep* or *awake;* and so on. Most of these terms must be avoided in a scientific description of behaviour" (p.6).

To replace this language with more scientific terms, Skinner introduced into the world of psychology the terms *stimulus, response,* and *reflex.* These had the advantage of being observable, quantifiable (i.e., countable), and thus presenting some objectivity. Notions such as the descriptions of sense experience could not be part of scientific inquiry because they were not available to such observation in the same way. The result was a reductionistic, thinly described story of who and what human beings were and led to a deterministic view of humans as always reacting to stimuli. This is most vividly illustrated in his novel, *Walden Two* (1962), in which he describes a behaviourally engineered utopia.

By way of contrast, phenomenological psychologists understand these sense descriptions to be precisely the stuff of the description of human experience. This language that Skinner rejected is precisely what we need to use to understand for ourselves and to share with one another the knowledge that we gain about being human. This language is historically and culturally rooted, its meaning is broadly shared, and when we talk like this, we "get it." Our dialogical conversations that use words and language which are shared in our contexts result in understandings of one another, and the development of communities that are rich beyond what Skinner envisioned in *Walden Two.* To be sure, Skinner provided many valid observations about how we respond but failed to take into account the unpredictability of human responses. We are not just stimulus responders. We think and reflect and decide to respond in ways not expected. As has been said in many places in trauma work, "no one is a passive recipient of trauma."

Dahl and Boss (2005) in their chapter on phenomenological research in the text by Sprenkle and Piercy (2005), *Research Methods in Family Therapy, Second Edition,* describe the importance of context for the experience of knowing. Knowledge begins with the sensate experience and is socially constructed as these experiences are shared in a commonly understood language. We may add that even Skinner's terms (*stimulus, response* and *reflex*) share this quality of social construction. We need a language that allows the researcher to be immersed in that which is being researched, and this common language does that.

Farnsworth (1985) presents these ideas about phenomenological psychology as an approach to psychology that is amenable to the task of integrating psychological and theological ideas in the service of the ministry of counselling. He then describes an *experiential theology*, as described in the theology of Jonathan Edwards and Rudolph Otto. Edwards, in reaction to the rationalistic bias of his time, which separated "unruly affection" from "sober reason" instead spoke of "passionate reason" balanced by "intellectual affection" (p.67). This experiential language provided a basis on which to understand faith from its experiential side. Farnsworth speaks of "receptivity" to actual communication from God. "Religious experience ... was a process of responding to an objective God outside of oneself with a feeling concerning him and what he has communicated" (p.69). This approach to theology makes it possible to understand human experience from both a psychological point of view and a theological point of view, and to integrate them through the commonalities the two languages share.

To counter the argument that this leaves us only with descriptions of subjective experience, we comment that there is nevertheless something to be experienced. From the theological side, there is God, revealed to us in the account about His Son, Jesus Christ. From the psychological side, there is a world of objects including other people, with whom we have to relate. Phenomenological psychology and experiential theology have as much to do with how we know what there is to know as simply with what is known. The hermeneutical questions this raises are also surely necessary to consider, and this reminds us of the discussion about the distinction between epistemology and ontology in the later chapter on narrative therapy.

Deborah van Deusen Hunsinger in her writings, *Theology and Pastoral Counselling: A New Interdisciplinary Approach* (1995) developed such an approach to the integration of the two languages, psychology and theology. "When God acts, it is within the events of ordinary human reality, which can also be described empirically and therefore psychologically." There are limits however, according to Hunsinger, as to what psychological language can describe:

> "Faith's perception of God's action cannot, of course, be described as such psychologically, but the ordinary human decisions and actions done within the context of everyday reality can. From a Barthian standpoint, any such complex occurrence can be viewed as having both a visible (psychological) dimension in the human being's decisions and actions, and, yet, also an invisible dimension in God's action, as perceived and attested by faith" (p.97f).

Thus, she claims that the two languages cannot be translated into each other. While they may speak of the same events, the language of faith is not susceptible to easy translation into the language of psychology.

Critical integration is the kind of integration that Jay Adams (1970) uses in his dismissal of all things psychological, and the kind which Gary Collins (2000) and Larry Crabb (2013) use in their notion of "spoiling the Egyptians."

In contrast, Farnsworth states,

> "(E)mbodied integration ... does not elevate theology to a position above the other disciplines, nor does it restrict the scope of integration to the intellectual. It is an emphasis on

all the disciplines equally and on Christian living at least as much as on Christian thinking. (It) is further differentiated from critical integration in that it focuses on the mechanics of research methodologies and is therefore scientific in orientation. Critical integration … focuses on the assumptions that underlie research methodologies, which makes it a more philosophical orientation. Another difference is that critical integration looks for specific psychological conclusions that are incompatible with a more general Christian worldview; embodied integration looks for specific psychological and theological conclusions that are comparable with each other. The emphasis of the former on points of tension stands in sharp contrast with the emphasis of the latter on points of similarity" (p.91).

Farnsworth's final chapter in *Whole-hearted Integration* is on the reality of truth, the bible, and the person. He describes an integration, then, that is incarnational, that grows out of the experienced interaction of the counsellor with the ideas of psychology, in a stance of obedient and dialogical listening to the tenets of Scripture, in the context of the work of counselling. Thus, integration is not complete until it comes together in the person-of-the-counsellor sitting in conversation with the person/s consulting with her or him.

Yet another view on the approaches to integration of psychology and theology is given by Beck and Demerest (2005). They cite G. R. Peterson who described three styles of integration as lenses to view theology: reductionism, challenge, and psychology. *Reductionism* reduces one completely into the categories of another. The result of this is that either theology or psychology is essentially lost. *Challenge* is the process of calling things in one discipline into question from the perspective of the other. This style exists in the evangelical world, mainly in the form of critiquing psychology with scriptural principles but "doing little else with the findings of this social science" (p.21). *Psychology*, the third model of integration, uses the cognitive sciences as a lens through which to view theology. None of these three—reductionism, challenge, or psychology—provide an adequate integration

Beck and Demerest (2005) then suggest a fourth model, *engagement*. This approach assumes that both psychology and theology produce important information for "the task of understanding the human person" (p.22). The result is the building of "working alliances" between the findings of science and the teachings of the bible. The result is a kind of teamwork between the two, which is open to adjustment, particularly since the findings of psychology are subject to change, and often rapid change.

A caveat here is necessary—and that is that we who are in the people-helping professions in this era, and as such, acting responsibly, must recognize how our learnings of psychology will serve as lenses to interpret the texts of scripture. In my own case, I recall the excitement I felt after learning Bowen Family Systems Theory, particularly the notion of multigenerational transmission process (see the chapter on family systems theory for a further explanation) and then in my bible reading coming to the genealogies in the Old Testament and reading them with a new awareness of the family context in which the entire bible story is told. This illustrated for me how a learning from a social science opened my understanding of scripture to new possibilities. We bring ourselves, complete with our narratives about our lives, into our reading of the scriptures. The same can be said of our "reading" of our clients' narratives as we engage with them.

This discussion must include a recognition of the breadth of work that has been done in the area of the integration of psychology and theology, sometimes more broadly described as psychology and Christianity. In 2000, Eric L. Johnson and Stanton L. Jones published *Psychology and Christianity: Four Views*. A chapter by Gary Collins shows how a committed Christian can have a positive view of the value of psychology in the work of therapy "because of its commitment to understanding people" (Collins, p.110). A decade later, a new edition was published, *Psychology and Christianity: Five Views*. Collins' chapter has disappeared, but his point of view is represented by other authors. (I suppose the world awaits, somewhat breathlessly, for *Psychology and Christianity: Six Views*.)

As Collins stated, "every effort at integration is a reflection of the integrators." This book presents only one view, but I hope that as you read these pages that you will catch some of the excitement and vigour that people who have sought to integrate these two fields have brought to the effort. My hope is that you, the reader, will reflect at length on these ideas and recognize their usefulness in your own people-helping work.

Overall, the field is recognizing the importance and value of integrative approaches to the work of psychotherapy. "As couple and family therapy (CFT) training programs begin to encourage more integrative approaches to therapy, researchers have identified the importance of punctuating the influence of common factors in treatment across models such as client factors, therapist factors, the therapeutic alliance, hope, common interventions, therapist allegiance to their model, and feedback." (Bartle-Haring et al, 2022, p.1200).

The integrated model as it will be described in the remainder of this book begins with a biblical anthropology based on the *imago Dei* concept given in the creation account. In our individualistic western culture, we tend to understand the image of God as applying to each human being individually. That's only half the story. The other half is that it is also a communal idea, in that the whole human race collectively bears the image of God. In his book, *The Doctrine of Humanity,* Charles Sherlock stated that the communal aspect is "theologically prior" to the individual aspect. This will be addressed further in the next chapter.

The communal aspect of humanity gives the theological grounding for a systemic and relational understanding of humanity. Family systems theory provides the behavioural content for this aspect. We are formed as people persons in the context of relationships with others, most immediately our families-of-origin, secondly in our local communities, and then in the societies in which our communities exist. The particular family theory we will consider in this book is one developed by psychiatrist and family therapy pioneer, Murray Bowen. The individual aspect of humanity provides the theological grounding for understanding our individual capacities. This aspect of who we are is often called the *psychodynamic aspect.* In a later chapter, we will explore the four human capacities as described by Larry Crabb in his *Understanding People,* namely, our fundamental motivations as human beings for belonging and mattering, our behaviours, our thoughts, and our emotions.

These two standpoints, the communal and the personal, provide the ontology for our work. Essentially, this is about how people function in the context of their relational contexts. While these are rich areas of inquiry, they do not include the epistemology. That is, having this body of fascinating knowledge doesn't equip us, by itself, to be able to enter a counselling conversation. For that, we turn in the final chapter to the practices of narrative therapy.

Narrative therapy is one of the so-called postmodern therapies in that it considers and deconstructs the contexts in which problems develop and are sustained. Practices of narrative therapy include externalizing the problem so that the person gains an identity apart from it, thereby recognizing intention and agency regarding the problem, and then growing to a new identity conclusion.

CHAPTER 3

Biblical Anthropology: A Biblical Understanding of Human Persons

My brother, Steve Berg, is a poet who reflects on the meaning of life through his written work. His poem *"Significant Strides in Soul Spotting."* (Berg, S.T., (2020) presents a particular theology of humanity that questions some orthodox beliefs about who we are as human beings, and how we are to view ourselves. I present it here because I believe our biblical anthropology requires a remake.

> *We have it on forensic authority that the ache in your heart can be filled with sunlight; the gnawing doubt about acceptance can be traced to the doorstep of your Grade two teacher; and your nail-biting habit, when tested against a forest walk, in combination with wren song, can be overcome.*
>
> *Mind you, we're in the early going and there's much about your internal map and pre-cellular structure that remains*

unexamined, and in the interest of scientific and intellectual honesty, we want to inform you that a substantial percentage, of what at this locus we'll call, your crux, may finally elude us.

You might, however, take comfort to know we've discarded the old model (frankly a bust). Replacing the reams of once resolute thought—to wit: the soul is individually and painstakingly crafted, packaged and housed by an Almighty Being; awaits embryonic enjoinment and arrives with an original flaw—will be, as our researchers have exhausted themselves to illuminate, an alternative and more radical understanding; far more fluid and too susceptible yet to observational influence to posit a full theorem, but holding potential in its vast layered Wonder, evident Mystery, if you will, of an open partnership in an unfolding creation.

Most surprising are the substrings of information coming back from experiments done on the ventromedial root of your animating essence. And on this, dear subject, if you'll allow, may I, on behalf of our team, tell you what an honour it is to be born on earth and take our place here with you: the kindness, the radiant selflessness, the joyous compassion, peace-loving wisdom and plain goodness that lies latent within, is nothing short of what we in the lab call, Nobel-worthy.

The only thing that remains, for the trial, is your cooperation in embracing that latency, then (the imperative) continually giving it away. The apparatus we've developed, while immensely complex, may yet be too crude to detect the emergent gleam of presence, of being of true-soul, yet, our methods stand, as you may be privy to see, on a hard-won hypothesis, effulgent with promise.

To me, the poem speaks of a hopefulness about who we are as people in community that provides an alternative to the deficit understanding that has been handed down to us through a couple of millennia of Christian theology; a replacement for the pathology-driven medical model that serves as the starting point for counsellors. He writes, "we have discarded the old model." What I hope to show in this chapter is that the "new" model actually predates the "old" and serves as a theological foundation for our work. This theological foundation is shaped by the biblical idea of the *image of God*.

A. The Importance of a Biblical Anthropology

Emil Brunner has said, what "gives the doctrine of man its peculiar significance, is the fact that all political, social and cultural development presupposes an 'anthropology'; that every political or social theory, and every social or political postulate stems from a definite anthropology" (Brunner, 1952, p. 47.) This chapter, on who we are as humans, individually and communally, provides the "foundation" of the integrated model. According to Jay Haley (1996), there are three things a therapist must know: who human beings are, how problems develop, and how people change. This chapter deals with the first of these.

To know about the image of God, we must know about the God of the image. Clark Pinnock (1996), in his book *Flame of Love: A Theology of the Holy Spirit*, writes this about the Spirit and Trinity (pp.29ff).

> "The trinity was revealed when the Father, seeking to show his love for lost humanity, communicated with us through Word and spirit. From this divine saving activity, we are given insight

into the inner life of God and glimpse a reciprocal community of love between Father, Son and Spirit, three persons relating in distinctive patterns. Note that this yields a different understanding of 'person' than is common in Western culture, where *person* is equated with the individual. For Descartes, a person is a thinking individual, and in his view social relationship does not enter the picture. The human is defined as an individual substance of rational nature, not as a person related to other persons essentially. But *person* when seen in the context of the Trinity signifies relationality. The divine Persons exist in relationship with others and are constituted by those relations. They are individuals in a social matrix" (p.30).

These ideas are supported with the following biblical texts.

B. Significant Biblical Texts

There are only three Old Testament texts that give us the phrase, "image of God":

Genesis 1:26ff - "Let us make mankind (*adam*) in our image, in our likeness ... So God created man in his own image, in the image of God he created him; male and female he created them."

The Hebrew word that is translated "mankind" here is transliterated as "adam," which developed into the proper name Adam. My parenthesis *adam* is the transliteration of the Hebrew word translated here as mankind. It includes not just the male but the whole human race. The feminine form of this word is *adamah* which means ground. Thus, the *adam*, the human race has its source in the *adamah*. It is a short step from this biblical idea to the term "mother earth."

Genesis 5:2,3 - "When God created man, he made him in the likeness of God. Male and female he created them, and he blessed them and named them Man (*adam*) when they were created. When Adam had lived 130 years, he fathered a son in his own likeness, after his image, and named him Seth.

Genesis 9:6 - In the image of God has God made man.

In the *Doctrine of Humanity,* Sherlock writes, "At three critical junctures in the pre-history of the race, the bible emphasizes that the human race is created in the image of God." Yet, the "image" is not defined. We are given neither a definition nor a description. J. Richard Middleton in his book, *The Liberating Image: The Imago Dei in Genesis 1,* describes the use of the term in Mesopotamian and Egyptian ancient literature. He writes,

> "…careful exegesis of Genesis 1:26–28, … does indeed suggest that the *imago Dei* refers to human rule, that is, the exercise of power on God's behalf in creation. This may be articulated in two different, but complementary, ways. Said one way, humans are *like God* in exercising royal power on earth. Said in another way, the divine ruler *delegated* to humans a share in his rule of the earth" (p.88).

There is an analogy from the practice of conquerors setting up an image of themselves in the conquered land. When the conquered people saw the image of the conqueror, they would know who their ruler was, because they had his "image" in their midst. Thus, we understand the expression "image of God" to be representational. The image of God is present in creation in the form of the human race. This excludes then any kind of anthropocentric understanding of the image of God as possessing the qualities of mind, emotions, etc. It portends something much more profound and far-reaching.

What does it mean to be created in the image of God? What is our function as representatives of the Creator. I suggest three responsibilities:

~ *Dependence*: We recognize our own dependence on the creation for our existence. While we represent the Creator in creation, we are also very much a part of the creation. We live and move and have our being in it. We depend on it for the sustenance of our own lives.

~ *Allegiance*: We owe our loyalty to the Creator whom we represent. In Luke 20, Jesus tells a parable of a ruler who let out his vineyard to tenants who proved disloyal and sought to claim ownership of the vineyard. In contrast to those tenants, our authority as representatives is a delegated one. This delegated authority is reflected in the command at creation that we are to "rule over" the rest of creation (Gen. 1:26). This is not a role we assume but one which we as the human race are given. There is an ongoing discussion about the use and the misuse of the idea of ruling over the rest of creation. The biblical account is one of stewardship and care for the creation, rather than exploitation of it.

~ *Accountability*: We are ultimately accountable to the Creator for the performance and results of our role as the representative race. This is implied in the command to "be fruitful and multiply," to fill the earth, and subdue it.

C. Embodiment

Gen. 2:7 states, "Then the LORD God formed the man of dust from the ground and breathed into his nostrils the breath of life, and the man became a living creature." We have here the fascinating picture of the coming together of dust and breath, indeed the physical and the spiritual. The word "breath" translates the Hebrew *"Ruach"* which can be translated as breath, wind, or spirit. As such it corresponds quite fully to the Greek *"pneuma"* of the New Testament. The dust of the earth is combined with the "breath of life" and the man becomes a *"nephesh."*

Much ink has been splashed in the discussion of the so-called bipartite or tripartite views of who we are as humans. Are we a body with a soul, or a body with a soul and a spirit? These views both come out of a Greek platonic worldview which sees a reality above the one in which we live. The Hebrew word *nephesh* doesn't allow for this bi (or tri)furcation but give us the notion of being a person as a singular whole. Perhaps it corresponds better to the German *mensch* which includes nuances difficult to capture in English. So, I posit here a view of human beings as unitary. We can use terms like *sociopsychoculturospiritual* ... and however much further we want to stretch this agglutinated term. The point is that we are unitary beings. I only go where my body takes me. Or, everywhere I go, I am there in body. The most sublime spiritual experience we may have involves physical involvement. Everything we experience happens in tissue. Synapses are synapsing, neurons are transmitting, and hormones are doing whatever hormones do.

Neuroscience has been contributing profoundly to this unitary way of understanding ourselves. They have discovered how our brains connect with other brains. The work of Daniel Stern, Peter Levine, Stephen Porges, Bessel van der Kolk, and many others have contributed marvelously over the past few decades to our understanding of how our "little gray cells" (to quote Hercule Poirot of Agatha Christie fame) are involved in our everyday life. I will leave it to you, the reader, to research each of these names if they are unfamiliar to you. Each of them has made a profound addition to our understanding of what it means to be a human being, a *mensch.*

D. Sexuality

Included in the creation account is the fact that we were created "male and female." We observe here the fundamental equality that the two sexes bear as created beings. In Genesis 2:21-25, some biblical interpreters have taken the account of the woman being taken out of the side of the man as showing a hierarchy. This earlier statement here in Genesis 1 precludes that. The point of the Genesis 2 account is not hierarchy but companionship, of the kind that results in the two being "one flesh" (v.25), another expression of equality. While I am on the subject, the "male and female" expression is quoted by Paul in Galatians 3:26, "There is no longer Jew nor Greek, slave nor free, male *and* female" (emphasis mine), where he describes being "in Christ" as erasing all class and caste distinctions in the church. (Many translations harmonize the three by translating the Greek *kai* as "nor" rather than the more accurate "and" of the Greek text. A better translation is simply to allow the "and" to stand indicating the adjustment to the distinction between male and female that is being made in the church which is the new "image" in creation.

Much damage has been done to women and to the witness of the church by how some have presented a hierarchical interpretation.

In his *A Brief History of Misogyny: The World's Oldest Prejudice*, Jack Holland presents a masterful and disturbing history of hatred towards women. He critiques both the Greek and Judeo-Christian "creation myths" as placing women as inferior to men (p.278) and bases his understanding of equality functionally in evolution and philosophically in the Enlightenment (p.282). I believe that we can make an even stronger case for equality from the biblical texts when understood from a creational perspective. They were created "male and female" in the "image of God."

There is a further consideration of the "and" that connects male and female in these texts. Consider the provocative book by Megan deFranza, *Sex Difference in Christian Theology: Male, Female, and Intersex in the Image of God*, in which she calls attention to the fact that not all humans are born clearly male or female. She defines intersex as: "ambiguous genitalia, congenital disjunction of internal and external sex anatomy, incomplete development of sex anatomy, sex chromosome anomalies, and disorders of gonadal development" (p.24), and that the frequency of such births is as high as between one in 2000 and one in 4500 births (p.45), as estimates vary depending on the researchers' definitions. She calls attention to how decisions about what to do with such people are culturally influenced as much as medically guided. Her main thesis is simply, "Male, female, and intersex persons are all created in the image of God, and all called to be conformed to the image of Jesus" (p.288). In this, she pleads for an acceptance of intersex people as they are, at least as the starting point of our responses to their needs. She is critical of the stance taken by evangelicals Stanley Grenz (1997) and Dennis Hollinger (2009) who accept the male-female binary as the creational norm that is divinely given (DeFranza, p.164). She cites Hollinger's conclusion that intersex people should seek medical help to "rectify" their bodies to conform to such norms. In taking a stance against this non-acceptance of intersex people, she cites Matthew 19:11-12: "For there are eunuchs who have been so from birth, and there are eunuchs who have been made eunuchs by men, and there are eunuchs who have made themselves eunuchs for the sake of the kingdom of heaven. Let the one who is able to receive this receive it." She stated that "much like the term 'intersex,' 'eunuch' was an umbrella concept—a word to cover a range of phenomena wherein humans did not measure up to the male ideal" (p.68).

As one more reference, *Life Isn't Binary: On Being Both, Beyond and In-between* by Meg-John Barker and Alex Iantaffi (2019) argue for radical inclusiveness in which we think beyond the binaries with which we divide our worlds. We need to be wary of binaries; I do not believe that we can have intelligent conversations without them, but it's essential that we be aware of both how they promote and obscure possibilities of understanding. The space between our notions of black and white allows for a broad range of shades of gray.

We need to be wary of the ways in which a strict binary view of human sexuality may obscure for us the reality of any particular client with whom we meet. One of the most obvious observations I make when I first meet with a client is whether this is a man or a woman. Another is whether he or she is old or young. While a simple black and white world might be easier to navigate, that binary may obscure an infinite range of very attractive grey and other hues, all of which contribute to this fascinating discipline of counselling in which we are engaged.

E. Human Beings as Communal Beings

The relational quality of being human is presented in Genesis 2:18: "It isn't good for the man to be alone." Interestingly, this contrasts with the pronouncement at the end of the creation process where all of creation is pronounced to be "very good." Here, the need for relationship is highlighted. This corresponds profoundly to a significant biblical theme of the people of God as a community. In the Old Testament, we see the people of Israel. In the New Testament, in Ephesians 1-3, there is reference to the church as being a body, a temple, and a family.

In a fascinating article on the relationship between neurobiology and psychotherapy, Andreas Manteufel (2005) provided a description of the social and relational requirements we have for our personal human development. His article, *Chromosomen non est omen – On the Relationship Between Neurobiology and Psychotherapy,* describes what has come to be called *the social brain.* The Latin phrase, *Chromosomen non est omen,* translates as "chromosomes are not a sign" and calls into question old understandings of genetic determinism. Here are four significant quotes from the article:

"Neurobiologists reject the existence of a central control, something like a 'central Ego'" (p.72).

"The regulation of genes is first and foremost situation-dependent and not hereditary. It depends on the actual contexts of each cell and also of the whole organism" (p.73).

"Changeaux has coined the term 'neurosociology' to describe society as a network of innumerable closely connected brains

(Changeaux, 2003). The intrapsychic system can be understood in social terms, as well. The so-called 'egoistic gene' has to incorporate itself into the 'society of genes'" (p.74).

"(M)irror neurons are ... specialized neurons (that) store the observations of patterns of movement of other people in a way that the observer can reproduce them (in the case of an infant, for example, a sound or mimicked movement). So, mirror neurons are an important foundation for learning by imitation" (p.74).

We now have a biological basis for the human community and the literature supporting the concept is growing apace. Seikkula et al (2018) describe "the human mind as a relational entity." They cite Daniel Stern, a developmental psychologist and author of *The Interpersonal World of The Infant: A View from Psychoanalysis and Developmental Psychology.* "The psychoanalyst Daniel Stern saw the new results as a 'revolution' (Stern, 2007, 36). Stern highlights the notion of the mind as an entity formed in relation to other minds, and—crucially—as formed through the sensory motor activity of the body" (p.856).

This recognition of the essential communal leads to the consideration of several other topics necessary for understanding who human beings are.

First, it invites a profound broadening of our understanding of health and healing. Dueck and Byron (2011) in an article on recovering from disasters in collectivist societies cite Wendell Berry (1995), "The community—in the fullest sense: a place and all its creatures—is the smallest unit of health and that to speak of the health of an isolated individual is a contradiction in terms" (p.245). We "live and move and have our being" (Acts 17:28) in the communities to which we belong. Ultimately, healthy people are such as they belong to healthy communities.

The essential communal provides another counter to the theological debate over whether we are bipartite or tripartite beings. That is. whether we are beings with a physical and a mental-spiritual aspect, a duality—or beings with a body, soul and spirit. Each of these words are used in scripture (at least in the English translations), but they are not given there with the kind of psychological definitional precision our modern era calls for and which expositors have sought to read into them. The differentiation between the mind and body, or soul and body is a linguistically constructed one that doesn't reflect the kind of inter-relational processes that recent neuroscientific finds are demonstrating. There is no allowance for the Platonic bifurcation as has been common in Christian theology ever since Platonic philosophy was introduced.

The concept of the communal raises for us also the fascinating and vital matter of culture. Culture is the result of humans living in community. Culture is defined generally as the sum-total of all human interactions in a particular time and place. A Google search demonstrates the breadth (and difficulty) of defining the term *culture.* This raises for the Christian psychotherapist a double challenge: first of understanding the role of culture in our work, and secondly, the task of what has come to be called "multi-cultural competence" in our work.

A great way to address the first challenge is through a review of the book, *Christ and Culture,* by H. Richard Niebuhr in which he discusses five historic approaches to culture by various Christian traditions. The approaches are "Christ against culture," "the Christ of culture," "Christ above culture," "Christ and culture in paradox," and "Christ the transformer of culture."

Christian psychotherapists are encouraged to read this book and reflect on their own understanding of how faith is to be lived out in their cultural context. It behooves us to reflect on Niebuhr's work, not just as counsellors, but also as citizens of our various communities and as members of our churches. In his *Concluding unscientific postscript*, Niebuhr states, "Our decisions are individual ... but they are not individualistic ... *We* are involved and every "I" confronts its destiny in *our* salvation or damnation (emphasis in the original) (p.243).

The second consideration, multi-cultural competence, is perhaps better stated as *multi-cultural sensitivity*. An excellent discussion of this is given in an article by A. G. Inman et al (2004.) The authors describe three aspects for consideration:

a. Sociopolitical awareness
b. Cultural sensitivity and knowledge
c. Cross-cultural conversational skills

Sociopolitical awareness involves understanding the current sociopolitical climate and its impact on clients from race-based cultural groups other than your own. This includes an understanding of the history of the group and its current location. Persons of African origin who are descendants of slaves will have a history and communal membership of which we need to be aware. Descendants of holocaust survivors, and refugees from around the world will have stories to share. It behooves counsellors to have a sufficient awareness of these histories to recognize when they become relevant in the counselling session. *Cultural sensitivity and knowledge* is the ability to empathize with a client's feelings and understand the interpersonal and environmental demands placed on the client. I recall meeting with an Indigenous client and getting a sense of the underlying anger that Indigenous people must feel as they consider the losses they have experienced especially with respect to the loss of land. I spoke of that awareness in the session. I said, "I can't understand why every First Nations person isn't seething with anger." He showed his appreciation by shaking my hand at the end of our meeting. *Cross-cultural conversational skills* refers to the use of appropriate communication skills and the ability to convey comfort within cultural difference.

For this multicultural sensitivity to be available to the counsellor, we need to add the terms *cultural humility* and *cultural curiosity*. Hook and Davis (2019) have edited a special issue of the *Journal of Psychology and Theology* devoted to the subject of cultural humility. They define *cultural humility* as follows:

"Cultural humility—expressed through openness to the other (Fowers & Davidov, 2006)—is the key virtue of the multicultural orientation framework. (It) has been defined using two main characteristics (Hook et al., 2013). First, on the intrapersonal dimension, cultural humility involves an awareness of one's limitation, both in regard to one's own cultural worldview (e.g., my cultural worldview is but one lens with which to view the world) and one's ability to understand the worldview of others (e.g., my ability to understand another individual's cultural background and experiences is limited). Second, on the interpersonal dimension, cultural humility involves an interpersonal stance that is other-oriented in relation to the other person's cultural background and experiences, marked by respect and lack of superiority" (p.72).

This stance of respect and lack of superiority can then also guide therapists' cultural curiosity as they encounter unfamiliar ideas and practices during a counselling conversation. Along with awareness of limitations, multicultural curiosity involves a readiness to ask questions of expressions or customs one doesn't understand, guided by a sensitivity as to the social permission and the clinical relevance of such a question. There is a delightful video of Insoo Kim Berg (1997) demonstrating solution-focused brief therapy with a family where the father states how his teen-age children need to "wake up and smell the coffee." Insoo, of Korean background, had never heard the expression before. In the video, she smiles and simply repeats the expression, and the father continues to describe his children's behaviour. Without understanding the phrase at the time, she continued the therapy session and later asked a colleague about the phrase's meaning. It would likely have been as effective for her to ask what it meant at the time of the session, recognizing to the father her different cultural background. On the other hand, it wasn't harmful to the meeting that she didn't ask.

In stark contrast, a papal bull issued by Pope Nicholas in 1455 describes how the European explorers were to view and treat the non-Christian Indigenous peoples, that is, "To invade, search out, capture, vanquish, and subdue all Saracens and pagans and to place them into perpetual slavery and to take their property" (Derrick, 2017). The ethical and moral implications of such attitudes are also demonstrated by J. Daschuk's extensively researched *Clearing the Plains: Disease, Politics of Starvation, and the Loss of Aboriginal Life* (2013).

Factors of awareness for psychotherapists that influence multicultural competence include worldview, theoretical orientation, value system, cultural group membership, and previous experience.

The third consideration under the topic of the human community is the change in viewpoint that a communal understanding of human being provides. Dueck (1995) provided a helpful perspective on this, listing the "five dimensions of individuality"— uniqueness, autonomy, privacy, self-sufficiency, and worth (p.96f). He reframes each of these in relational and communal terms. This reframed understanding is much more conducive to a relational and flexible approach to the work of psychotherapy. The individualistic value of *uniqueness* is reframed in terms of being *members of a body* (1 Corinthians 12:27). "Nowhere in the story of the Hebrews or the Christian church is uniqueness taken as an end in itself. Diversity is not valued apart from unity" (p.115). While diversity of gifts is acknowledged and celebrated, it is the membership in the community that is valued. Likewise, the value of *autonomy* is reframed by the value of *accountability*. Autonomy implies independence. "From the nature of a covenant relationship with Yahweh and fellow members in the covenant, one derives accountability to God in the midst of a people. To be accountable means to give account. It is important for the sake of relationships to interpret our actions to our brothers/sisters," (p.116).

The third value Dueck lists is that of *privacy*. This is reframed in terms of the importance of *community*. Privacy "assumes a dichotomy between self and society. In contrast to this separation, the biblical story assumes the essentially social nature of humanity," (p.117). "The communal nature of the personhood leads to ... (seeing) relationships within the church community as openness, intimacy, and dialogue. Love is the glue that gives coherence to community" (p.118). Our individualistic culture obscures the value and necessity of community in our formation and the sustaining of life. It is acknowledged, of course, that a strong communal culture can also be oppressive. As a student from a communal culture stated, "My own cultural background influenced me to think in a communal sense rather than to focus on individuals. I came to recognize that my culture easily ignores the individual's needs and dignity. It was familiar for me to respect the rules by the majority," (Younjou Seo, 2010). Nevertheless, a healthy community is expressed by Taniguchi (2005) who used the Japanese word *jibun* for a sense of self to describe this. This word consists of two parts, *ji,* which implies self, and *bun,* which implies portion. That is, *self* in Japanese culture means "one's portion," which suggests that the self is also always a part of the group. In other words, in Japanese culture, the self does not exist without the group to which it belongs.

The fourth concept, *self-sufficiency,* is reframed as *reconciliation.* "In contrast to self-actualization, self-realization, and self-fulfillment, Jesus assumed that personal development comes only through self-sacrifice, dedication to the calling of reconciliation. Self-affirmation, personhood, and wholeness are a result of sacrifice of self. Paul suggests that personal integrity may not always be as important as the needs of a fellow Christian. To order one's life by the weaker person is the example of love rather than integrity and the basis of the creating of community" (p 118). The self-psychology that individualistic popular psychology (pop psychology) has given us, e.g., self-esteem, self-worth, self-actualization, etc., is reframed here in terms of a person's contribution to and participation in the life of the community.

The popular understanding of the second great command, that we should love our neighbour as ourselves, is that we must first love ourselves in order to love our neighbour. This individualistic understanding of the command is overturned when one considers that the command to love the neighbour comes first and the love of self is a product, not a pre-requisite of love of neighbour. This also presents a strong critique of Abraham Maslow's hierarchy of needs, in which "self-actualization" is the ultimate goal of a fulfilled life and is stated as a need. The assumption is that all the lesser needs must be fulfilled in order for the final one to be achieved. Author of *The Will to Meaning*, Viktor Frankl (1969), posits "self-transcendence" (p.18) instead. This is the ability to focus attention on doing something for the sake of others, as opposed to *self*-actualization, in which doing something for oneself is an end goal.

The fifth concept, *worth*, Dueck reframes as *love*. "While the sanctity and worth of the individual are recognized, the individual life is not seen as an end in itself" (p.119). The "disciple community" emerges from the story of Jesus. "It is a community that is to be characterized by humility, reconciliation, a thirst for justice, and love. The church is the extension of this disciple community" (p.119). To quote Frankl again, in "the capacity of self-transcendence … man transcends himself either toward another human being or toward meaning. Love … is that capacity which enables him to grasp the other human being in his very uniqueness (p.18f).

These five reframes are a way of understanding who human beings are as they exist as people in community. They provide an essential corrective to the individualistic perception that we have inherited in our culture, and they correspond with the understanding of humanity that provides a much richer way of engaging in conversation with people who have come to consult with us.

F. Human Beings as Originally Good

To complete this chapter, a discussion of the sinfulness of humankind is needed. Theology points to Genesis 3 and the account of what theologians have come to call "the Fall." We have fallen from innocence, from an intimate relationship with our Creator, from life in paradise, and have come under the curse of sin. Five-point Calvinism, expressed in the acronym TULIP begins with "total depravity" as the starting point in its succinct description of what it considers to be essential Christian theology. "Original sin" is the term that Augustine gave the church in his writing, based on such verses as Psalm 51: 5 – "Surely I was sinful at birth, sinful from the time my mother conceived me." Paul's extensive description of sin in Romans 1:18-3:20 which concludes with the statement: "There is no one righteous, no not one," in which he quotes Psalm 14. Essentially, the doctrine of sin, hamartiology, is an essential feature of Christian theology and the starting point for the Christian view of who human beings are.

It has its counterpoint in psychotherapy, as seen in its practice based on the medical model. This model states that the psychotherapist begins with an assessment, a description of the presenting problem and then diagnosed according to a nosology of some sort, most popularly the *Diagnostic and Statistical Manual of Mental Disorders*.

Thus, from both standpoints, theology and psychotherapy, the understanding of who human beings are begins with the Problem. The person is the Problem.

I want to provide what I believe is an essential corrective to this approach to the work of psychotherapy as well as to ministry in our churches. The problem should not be the starting point. This is not to deny the fact of sin. Reinhold Niebuhr, brother to H. Richard cited above, said, "Sin is the only Christian doctrine for which we have empirical evidence!" (Cited in Toews, 2013, p.90)

However, there are some voices that question this perspective. From the point of view of theology, Mark S. Smith (2019) has provided a review of the various interpretations that Old Testament scholars have given regarding what actually happened in the Garden of Eden when the man and the woman "fell." The point I want to make here is that original sin is not the original thing. The original thing, as given in Genesis 1, is goodness.

Therefore, I posit a different starting point than either Christian theology or the medical model of psychotherapy present, namely the idea of original goodness as the first understanding of who human beings are theologically, accompanied by a strengths-based view psychotherapeutically. The congruence of these approaches to therapy as practiced in narrative therapy will become evident later in the book.

I have written an article on the subject entitled *Can Christians do Narrative Therapy? Original Goodness instead of Original Sin as the Starting Point for Therapy and Theology* (Berg, 2015). I argue there for a theology of humanity that begins where the biblical narrative begins, with the original goodness emphasized there. This provides a basis for one of the premises of narrative therapy, that "the person is not the problem, the problem is the problem." The same premise provides for the several "strength-based" approaches to psychotherapy that have developed in recent years.

CHAPTER 4

The Systemic and Relational Approach to Psychotherapy: The Systemic Theory of Murray Bowen

The systemically and relationally oriented approach to therapy is founded on the communal and relational aspect of who we are as human beings. If it's true that we are biologically constituted to be in relationships, then our understanding of how to provide help to people must include, indeed begin with, an understanding of the ways in which people relate in their communities, beginning in the smallest community of which they are a part, their families. And if it is true that theologically the communal nature of "image of God" precedes the individual one, then we have the theological basis for understanding people from a relational and systemic perspective.

This chapter reviews the history and influences that produced the family systems movement, and then considers the contribution of

Murray Bowen, one of the significant pioneers of family therapy in the field of mental health. The chapter concludes with a discussion of the use of these ideas in the actual practice of psychotherapy.

A. Basic Systemic Concepts that Shaped Family Therapy

The family therapy movement began as a revolt and evolved into a revolution. It was a revolt against the orthodoxy of the psychoanalytic approach to psychotherapy that had developed out of the work of Sigmund Freud and his followers. The extensive time required for therapy and the expense involved made therapy unavailable for the vast majority of the population. There was also a growing dissatisfaction with the effectiveness of psychoanalytic work in bringing about the change that clients were seeking.

It was a revolution as the dogmas and ideologies of psychoanalytic and individualistic approaches were challenged and alternative approaches to the work of psychotherapy developed. One significant alternative was the observation that people were influenced by their relationships, especially with other members of their family. This revolutionary observation was that desired change could happen when relational patterns changed, not only when, or even rather than, change resulting from insight through psychoanalysis. An entertaining example of this is the edited book, *Paul Watzlawick: Insight May Cause Blindness and Other Essays* (Ray and Nardone, 2009). That shift was not without caution on the part of initial adopters. Many early family therapists embraced a rather clandestine approach to their conferencing as they would ask, almost in hushed tones, "Do you see families?" Gradually, they became bolder and began to publish papers and books. The first book published in the emerging field of family therapy was *Psychodynamics of Family Life* by Nathan Ackerman in 1958. The first issue of a leading journal in the field, *Family Process*, appeared in 1961. (Nichols and Davis, 2017).

While the psychoanalytic approach hasn't disappeared, it has taken a relational turn, as evidenced in a series of articles on the relational aspect of therapy published in 2023 in the *Journal of Psychology and Christianity*. An example of this is the article by Winston Seegobin, Racial Healing in the Church: The Usefulness of the Interpersonal Process in Therapy Model (42, 2, 116-126). Another even more cogent article is the one by Bland and Yoo in which these psychoanalytically oriented authors state the following:

> This relational revolution within psychoanalytic theory, and
> the accompanying emphasis on mutual, albeit asymmetrical,
> influence within the therapeutic relationship, pushes the
> integration project beyond a mere theoretical endorsement of
> relationality. The intersubjective reality of psychotherapy defeats
> any notion of a distantiated therapeutic objectivity, where
> the therapist knows and the patient does not. Consequently,
> the therapist, as co-participant and co-constructor of the
> therapeutic bond, may not rely exclusively on their theoretical
> or clinical knowledge/skill to navigate the relational terrain.
> They must explore and discover how they are contributing to
> the construction and elaboration of this terrain. If and when
> this exploration happens, every therapist quickly realizes that
> it is not just their theory that is at play and contributing to the
> therapy process. The person of the therapist—their spiritual/
> religious tradition, values and ethical frame, and personal

development within a given cultural context—all exert conscious and unconscious influence on every aspect of the therapeutic relationship. (Bland and Yoo, 2022, 238).

Among the sociocultural influences that has brought this realization of the importance of a relational and systemic lens to individualistic approaches has been that of family therapy and its relational and contextual understandings of human life. Much of the material in this chapter is drawn from the textbook by Michael P. Nichols and Sean D. Davis, *Family Therapy: Concepts and Methods, Twelfth Edition*, (2021) which is a good review of the field. The first edition of the text, published in 2001, was authored by Michael Nichols and Richard C. Schwartz.

One of the first influences for this revolutionary, relational turn was the development of *cybernetics theory*, the notion of circular rather than linear causation. A core concept is the notion of feedback loops. A negative feedback loop is a message to stop the action whereas a positive feedback loop is the message to repeat it. An example of a negative feedback loop is the thermostat in a heating system that turns the system off when the desired temperature is reached. An example of a positive feed back loop is addiction, where the satisfaction of the addictive substance or action leads to repetition. In this usage, negative and positive doesn't mean bad or good, but the effect of the action. Thus, positive feedback loops can reinforce destructive actions, whereas a negative feedback loop will return the organism or machine to homeostasis, as in the example of the home heating thermostat where the device will turn the furnace on or off to maintain a desired temperature.

On the other hand, negative feedback loops can leave the family system stuck in unhappy ways of relating. A family relational system develops a certain way of relating that feels comfortable and can become resistant to change, even though the change may be a desirable one. Thus, the family therapist's role is to interrupt the feedback system to make healthier interactions possible.

Closely related is the notion of *systems theory*, the idea that every system is made up of smaller systems and is also part of a larger system. Every person consists of many biological systems and may belong to many different social systems. The family will be part of a community system, and the community may be part of a nation. All these systems are acting upon each member system and are being acted upon by the member systems.

One interesting and practical example of this is described in Tomm et al. (2014). The authors' main thesis is the invitation to track sequences of actions and responses as therapists are meeting with a client, whether individually, or as a couple or family. They call their intervention the Interpersonal Patterns scope (IPscope) and define it as "a cognitive instrument for distinguishing and describing Interpersonal Patterns for systemic assessment" (p.18).

Problems that people encounter then are understood not to exist within a person's head or heart or body, but are sustained somehow in the system of interactions and relational patterns that the members of a system are in. The experience of depression for example is understood to be a function of such interactions. Therefore, a solution may be found in a change in the interpersonal interactions that the person is in.

A further addition to this way of thinking comes from the contribution of *social constructionism*. This is an outcome of the philosophy of constructivism that dates to Immanuel Kant who theorized that our minds are "filters through which we process and interpret the world" (p.94, 9th ed.). This idea was given an empirical basis when "studies of brain function showed that we can never know the world as it exists out there; all we can know is our subjective experience of it" (p.93f).

An exaggeration of these ideas is the notion that since we can only know our experience, there is then nothing else to be known. This is patently untrue; this simply says that whatever we know is limited. There does exist something that can be known beyond our experience; known due to the experience of others. The example of three blind men examining an elephant provides an illustration. One man touches the trunk and says an elephant is like a hose. Another has the tail and says it's like a rope. A third has an ear and says the elephant is like a piece of leather. The answer is not to debate who is right, but to recruit a large team of blind men so that the whole elephant can be examined. Then, when they put their notes together, they will have a reasonably accurate description of the elephant.

The recent development beyond the notion of constructivism is social constructionism. "Constructivism says that we relate to the world on the basis of our own interpretations. Social constructionism points out that those interpretations are shaped by the social context in which we live" (p.95). Each of the blind men will bring their own understanding of elephantology and in the scientific conversations that will follow their research, as they present their papers at their conferences, a society of elephantologists will develop a science about elephants that will enrich their research and hopefully their lives.

The application to therapy from these ideas is the process of deconstruction of problematic patterns and identity conclusions in order to construct healthier and more helpful ways of relating to and within the systems in which we live. This involves an examination of the social contexts, and the social discourses that constitute those contexts, with a view to evaluating and finding ways to live above them. Romans 12:2 says, "Do not conform any longer to the pattern of this world but be transformed by the renewing of your mind." It is the "patterns of this world" that constitute the sociocultural context in which we live. It is the deconstruction of those patterns that makes possible the renewing of our minds as they are freed from the tyranny of the discourses.

The postmodern movement has given rise to several approaches to therapy that take into account the social discourses that can give rise to problems in living that people experience. Narrative therapy is one such approach that specifically examines the "norming" discourses and questions their influence. The promise given is the "spacious place" (Ps. 18:19; 31:8) for living that such deconstruction permits.

B. History of the Early Family Therapy Movement

In addition to the systems and cybernetic influence described above, there were several other influences that contributed to the development of family therapy. These included the research into schizophrenia, the development of group psychotherapy, the child guidance movement, and the marriage enrichment movement.

Schizophrenia research was a significant challenge for the psychoanalytic approach to therapy. Most of the family therapy pioneers who were psychiatrists were involved in some way or other with investigating and seeking cures to this challenging puzzle. Very early in his career, Freud himself had speculated about the connection between schizophrenia and one's family of origin. But the most direct work in this area was done by Gregory Bateson at the Mental Research Institute (MRI) in Palo Alto, California. His interest was in patterns of communication. He observed that every communication act carries a content and a command. The content is the words spoken and the command is a function of the relationship between the two people. He called this command the metacommunication—the often-unvoiced expectation that the words carry. For example, a therapist might ask, "May I ask you a question?" At first glance, permission is simply being asked to question further. However, the context offers many possibilities. If the client has been talking non-stop, the command function may be, "May I interrupt?" If the client has just shared a heart-breaking story, the question may be a gentle entry into the silent space after the story. When there is an incongruence between the communication and the meta-communication, this could be confusing for the recipient who would have to choose between which of the two to respond to, thus ensuring that he would be wrong about the other one. The receiver would have to disobey one to obey the other. One example might be the mother who gave her son two neckties for his birthday. To show his appreciation, he wore one of them to dinner that evening, to which she commented, "What's the matter, didn't you like the other one?" As an exercise, we can reflect on the communication and meta-communication implications in this question from the mother.

Researchers who studied these patterns in families came up with a very uncomplimentary word for this, namely, the *schizophrenogenic mother.* The suggestion was that it was mothers in particular who would give these double-bind messages to their children. While there is a rich history of research and theorizing, and a great deal was learned about families and therapeutic approaches to working with families, this research in family systems in order to find a cause of schizophrenia did not result in a cure for schizophrenia—a condition which continues to be a challenge for the field.

Another source of theory and practice came out of the newly developing area of *group psychotherapy,* which has become a specialty in its own right. It is attractive because it promises efficiency that cannot be attained when meeting with one person at a time. It also promises effectiveness in that the group participants are being impacted not only by the therapist but also by the other group members. The "bible" on group psychotherapy was written by Irvin Yalom and entitled, *The Theory and Practice of Group Psychotherapy,* now in its sixth edition (2020). Significant work was done by people at the Tavistock Clinic in London, England, motivated by the war effort during WWII, both during the mobilization phase and later in the aftermath in caring for veterans. There were also many other developments in the USA, and elsewhere. One significant contribution from the area of group psychotherapy was the idea of the difference between *content* and *process.* Content was the topic of discussion, and process was the group dynamics that occurred during the discussion. This included observations about who responded to whom and such. Out of these observations grew the notion of *roles,* in which various group members each had different roles in the process. These ideas are still useful. It's easy for therapists, especially new ones, to get caught up in the content of the conflict a couple or family brings and to try to help them solve it. For example, the therapist might want to help them decide whose turn it is to take out the trash. That's dealing with content. Process involves the observation and engagement of the couple or family in the ways in which they are interacting, and the patterns in which they are caught. When that awareness grows, they can work out for the issues for themselves, including those around family chores such as taking out the trash.

Two other influences, child guidance and marriage counselling, were both more related to family life. Alfred Adler is the pioneer best known for his attention to working with children. The *child guidance movement* that came out of his work expanded significantly as his ideas grew in influence. Adler, a student of Freud, thought that good parenting practices would be an effective way of preventing adult mental health problems. His students included the influential American Rudolph Dreikurs whose work included the founding of the American Orthopsychiatric Association, whose mission was the healthy nurturing of children. Eventually, child guidance clinics were established in cities across North America. It is not a huge leap to move from caring for children to caring for children and their families. John Bowlby, who did his work at the Tavistock Clinic in London, is famous for his research on attachment theory, which has become an important part of many current approaches to psychotherapy, especially in its contribution to emotionally focused therapy. One of the most famous of these centres in the USA is the Philadelphia Child Guidance Clinic where family therapy pioneer Salvador Minuchin developed his structural family therapy approach to this work.

Marriage counselling also developed during the early part of the twentieth century. Among the early publishers and counsellors was the team of Hannah and Abraham Stone. Their book, *A Marriage Manual*, was first published in 1935 with the subtitle, *A Practical*

Guidebook to Sex and Marriage. Its 1953 revision included chapters on mate selection, fitness for marriage, sexual function and dysfunction, and a section on happiness and emotional and psychological problems in marriage relationships. The Stones established a clinic for working with couples in New York city, and others were also established in various other cities in the USA and other countries of the world.

One interesting idea that marriage counsellors dealt with was the notion of interlocking neuroses. Couples developed patterns of interacting based on the neuroses they brought into their marriages, and the idea that couples should therefore be treated concurrently. "Every neurosis in a married person is strongly anchored in the marital relationship. It is a useful and at time indispensable therapeutic measure to concentrate the analytic discussions on the complementary patterns and, if necessary, to have both mates treated" (Nichols, 2010, p.23, citing Mittleman, 1944, p.491). Again, it is a short logical step from these ideas to the notion of treating families as a whole.

Finally, we must mention, albeit too briefly, the tremendous influence of the field of *social work* and of *social workers* in the development of family therapy. Social work began in the nineteenth century when the social concerns arising out of the industrial revolution became apparent. This involved caring for basic physical needs as well as emotional distress and an effort to affect the social forces causing such problems. Social workers developed the practice of home visits, something pastors do, that medical doctors used to do, and family therapists are rediscovering. They understood the importance of the family unit and the social context in which the family unit existed. One early author was Mary Richmond who wrote *Social Diagnosis,* (1917) in which she described what she called *family cohesion.* She stated that the "emotional bonding between family members was critical to their ability to survive and flourish" (Nichols, 2010, p.16). Many of the family therapy pioneers including Virginia Satir, Insoo Kim Berg, Steve de Shazer, Michael White began their professional lives as social workers.

C. Early Pioneers of the Family Therapy Movement

The discipline of family therapy has a vibrant, decades-long history. This history is peopled by a diverse and creative group of pioneers on whose shoulders the profession stands. Their key contribution was the recognition of the importance of relationships in how we live our lives, beginning with the most fundamental of relationships—that of our families of origin. The field has been accompanied by the development of professional associations, journals, and conferences. And it continues to grow.

A brief study of the pioneers who led the development of family therapy as a profession is an interesting read. These individuals were creative, courageous, and learned how to work collaboratively with one another in spite of the fact that they lived in various parts of North America and Europe, and came from various professional disciplines. They attended and presented at each other's conferences, read each other's papers, had many personal conversations, cross-fertilizing ideas and concepts.

This section will provide a cursory review of each pioneer's contribution, followed by a separate section on Murray Bowen's contribution. For any of these pioneers that attract their interest, readers are encouraged to search out further information, especially any of their original publications. The influence of many of them continues as the field of family therapy burgeons.

Gregory Bateson - anthropologist, social scientist, cyberneticist

Gregory Bateson (1904-1980) was not a therapist in the usual sense. His initial discipline was anthropology, and that interest also connected him with the famous anthropologist, Margaret Mead, whose work among the people of Indonesia, particularly in Bali, won her world-wide acclaim. Bateson joined her in her research, and during that time, the two were also joined in marriage, a union that produced a daughter, Mary Catherine Mead, who became an anthropologist in her own right.

Bateson's primary interest and contribution to family therapy was his interest in communication theory. He did most of his work in this area with the people at the Mental Research Institute in Palo Alto, California, in their research with schizophrenia. Key ideas in this area of theory are the notions of *communication* and *metacommunication*. Every act of communication between two people persons contains content and some kind of report on the relationship between the two. This report aspect is what he referred to as metacommunication, i.e., the communication about the communication. For example, the words, "How are you?" have very different responses when asked by a counsellor of a counsellee and or two friends passing on the street. The metacommunication happens in two different social contexts, and thus is differently socially constructed—and because in both cases the pairs understand the cultural context, no further explanation is usually needed from either to explain. When it comes to multicultural competence, however, the metacommunication is often not as easily understood, and often further explanation is required.

Bateson's other contribution was the idea of the *double bind*, already described above in the story of the mother and the son with the two ties. When there is an incongruence between the communication and the metacommunication, the receiver must choose which one to respond to, and thus will always be wrong. The anxiety arising out of such a relationship context can be quite debilitating.

Bateson published several important books and articles, as well as made many scholarly presentations. A good primer of his work is in the collection of essays, *Steps to an Ecology of the Mind,* originally published in 1972. The second edition was published in 2000 and includes a foreword by his daughter, Mary Catherine Bateson. The first part of the book is entitled "Metalogues" which he defines as "a conversation about some problematic subject … such that not only do the participants discuss the problem, but the structure of the conversation as a whole is also relevant to the same subject" (p.1). We can appreciate in his definition of metalogues attention to both communication and metacommunication. This section of his book is a delightful collection of conversations that he has with his daughter about such "problems." The first is entitled, "Why to things get in a muddle?"

Daughter: Daddy, why do things get in a muddle?

Father: What do you mean? Things? Muddle?

Nathan Ackerman – psychiatrist, psychoanalyst

Nathan Ackerman (1908-1971) was a specialist in child psychiatry who began his career at the Menninger Institute in Houston, Texas. He eventually moved to New York where he started the Family Mental Health Clinic of Jewish Family Services and then the Family Institute, which was renamed the Ackerman Institute following his death in 1971. Currently, the Ackerman Institute for the Family continues to provide clinical services for families. It also offers training to clinicians in the practices of family therapies.

When he started at the Menninger Clinic, he conformed to the practice of seeing the child separately and then having someone else see the mother. However, he soon began to see both together, and thus began his foray into family therapy. After his move to New York, he became more and more active in seeing whole families. However, his psychoanalytic thinking continued to influence him. In the same way that psychoanalysts see their patients as people with defences that need to be overcome for a more flourishing life, he saw families as having defences. He described his therapeutic work as "tickling the defenses" (Nichols, 2010, p.31). As families overcame these defences, they became free to relate to each other in healthier ways. The family's defences could be observed in the behaviours and ways of relating directly, and were treated experientially in therapy, rather than being named and discussed in an effort to be objective about them. This approach was another harbinger of experiential therapy, in contrast to insight- based approaches. Because he kept his feet firmly in psychoanalytic ways of thinking as he developed his family therapy interventions, he has sometimes been called the "grandfather of family therapy."

His contribution to the literature about family therapy is his *Treating the Troubled Family*, published in 1966. It includes these topics: crisis and therapy, the question of cure, the family as a psychosocial entity, the breakdown of healthy process, the functions of the family therapist, treating husband and wife, child-oriented intervention, rescuing the scapegoat, and return to reality.

Carl Whitaker – experiential therapist; therapy of the "absurd"

Carl Whitaker grew up on a dairy farm in upstate New York, something that influenced his view of life and of psychotherapy. His medical studies led him first into obstetrics and gynecology, and then into psychiatry where he spent the rest of his career. After positions at the University of Louisville and Emory University, he spent ten years collaborating with a group of therapists, the result of which was *experiential psychotherapy*. In 1965, he moved to the University of Wisconsin at Madison where he remained until his retirement.

His fascination with the mind of schizophrenic patients led him away from the use of medication towards listening to their thoughts and ideas in order to understand them. His work contributed to a greater respect for his patients and a humble and amusing deprecation of the expertise of the therapist. For example, in a video he states, "One of my joys in this kind of racket is the psychotherapy I get from making you into my therapist … I think that anyone who tries to earn a living by helping people who are crazy when we're all just as crazy or crazier than they are, and we haven't been able to do anything about ourselves, you know, that's really pretty sick!" (Whitaker, 2023).

A touching story of his heart for families came to me in a private conversation. He had been invited to present at a conference sponsored by the family therapy program at Sioux Falls Seminary (my alma mater). He had been previously invited to present at the conference but had cancelled due to illness. He recovered in time and made his way to the conference venue. However, without informing Whitaker, the organizers had invited someone else to present. When he arrived at the conference, he learned he wasn't needed. Unfazed and un-insulted, he returned to the airport, where in the waiting room he encountered a family who were having a public disagreement. He engaged the family in a conversation and sought to provide what help he could in that situation. He and the family attracted an audience of the other travelers who gathered around and refused to board when their departure time came around because they wanted to see how it ended!

A good representation of his work is the book, *The Family Crucible: The Intense Experience of Family Therapy* (1978), co-authored with one of his students, Augustus Napier. It is a book-length case study of a family that Whitaker and Napier saw jointly. Whitaker believed that the work of family therapy was too emotionally intense to be done by only one therapist, and it wasn't until later in his life that he thought he was mature enough in his own emotional makeup to work solo with families.

Virginia Satir – family sculpting

Virginia Satir emphasized emotional experiencing as a key feature in family therapy. Her career took her from private practice in Chicago to the training program at the Illinois State Psychiatric

Institute and from there to the MRI in Palo Alto, California where Satir became the first director of training. She remained there until 1966, when she left to become the director of the Esalen Institute in Big Sur, California. She became a popular and sought-after conference presenter whose work featured seeing families in session and providing enactments involving placing family members in positions that represented their positions and roles in a family, and then re-arranging them to provide the experience of possibilities beyond their *stuckness,* the rigidity of the relational patterns She called this family sculpting.

One of her best-known publications is *Conjoint Family Therapy,* first published in 1978 and subsequently in 1983. It is a theoretical presentation of her work with families. In an earlier popularly written book, is *Peoplemaking,* in which she delineates styles of relating within families—namely, placating, blaming, computing, and distracting. A fifth style, leveling, is her term for maintaining healthy relationships. The first four are either one-up or one-down positions, whereas leveling sees oneself as the equal of the other without a need to manipulate oneself or the other. There are strong overtones to Bowen's concept of self-differentiation and to the biblical idea of "truthing in love" (Ephesian 4:15).

Salvador Minuchin – structural family therapy

Salvador Minuchin was born in Argentina. His career took him to Israel, New York, and finally to the Philadelphia Child Guidance Clinic where he developed his theories about the structure of families. His connections included people from the MRI in Palo Alto, particularly Jay Haley, who joined him in Philadelphia for a period. His ideas were developed primarily during his work with delinquent boys in New York and later in Philadelphia. He and his colleagues taught themselves to do family therapy. They developed the one-way window through which they could watch each other work. This became a feature of family therapy and family therapy training centres until the advent of electronic cameras and monitors.

His work with boys from troubled families led him to his theories about family structure. He observed that families could be *enmeshed* or *disengaged,* either of which could produce troubled family members. An ideal family was one in which roles were clear between family members and family subsystems, and there were healthy communication patterns between them. Family relationship patterns were inter-connected so a change by one family member, which he called first-order change, would not likely produce a desired outcome. A family system required second-order change, a change in the pattern of relating. A change toward a more engaged father and less enmeshed mother, away from a disengaged father and over-involved mother, could be produced in a process of family therapy in which such patterns could be made visible as they were experienced and enacted in session. As the patterns became visible to the family, especially the parents, they became accessible to change.

A major publication describing this work was *Families of the Slums; An Exploration of their Structure and Treatment,* coauthored with Braulio Montalvo and several other colleagues. A large body of literature was produced by many notable authors who were trained and who taught structural family therapy. It was the most widely practiced form of family therapy in the 1970s and 1980s.

Ivan Boszermenyi-Nagy – contextual family therapy

Ivan Boszermenyi-Nagy was of Hungarian descent and immigrated to the USA in 1950. His early training was in psychoanalysis, but he had the good fortune of being a student of Virginia Satir at the Illinois State Psychiatric Hospital, which led him to explore family patterns.

His particular contribution to the field of family therapy was the concept of ethical accountability. Among the drives that are involved in family relationships is the desire for justice, and the drive to right generational and other wrongs. These wrongs exist in the context of relationships within families and between families and their sociocultural contexts. As a result, family members may feel entitled or indebted, and these feelings will affect their relational patterns and practices.

The major work that describes his approach is *Invisible Loyalties: Reciprocity in Intergenerational Family Therapy*, co-authored with Geraldine Spark. An illustration of contextual family therapy is chapter four, "Justice and social dynamics." They write:

> "The reason for introducing justice as a major dynamic concept in family theory issues from the significance of loyalty patterns in the organization and regulation of close relationships. In order to conceptualize loyalty as a system force rather than merely as a disposition of individuals, we have had to consider the existence of an invisible ledger which keeps an account of past and present obligations among family members. … The individual family member … is born into a field of greater or lesser obligations. The fact that his parent and their ancestor

were all caught in similar expectations and had to balance filial with parental obligations makes it necessary to think of the ledger as a multigenerational structure. The structure of expectations makes up the fabric of loyalties and, together with the accounts of actions, the ledger of justice" (p.53).

While contextual family therapy has been much less influential in the development of the field, it nevertheless has an important place for the unique contribution it makes, both in its emphasis on a desire for justice, and for its multigenerational focus.

The Palo Alto group – strategic family therapy

A group of creative and provocative practitioners gathered in and around Palo Alto, California. The Bateson group was formed by Gregory Bateson when he received a grant in 1952 to study paradox in communication. He invited Jay Haley, John Weakland and Don Jackson to join him in this research. Each of these individuals went on to achieve fame in the field of family therapy in their own right. Jay Haley published *Learning and Teaching Psychotherapy*. He later moved to Philadelphia where he joined Salvador Minuchin for a time. He later teamed up Cloe Madanes to whom he was married for a while.

In 1959, Don Jackson formed the Mental Research Institute (MRI) in Palo Alto, California to formalize the ideas and practices that Bateson and his associates had been developing. He invited Richard Fisch, Jay Haley, John Weakland, and Paul Watzlawick, a creative gathering of like-minded therapists who saw personal problems as having a larger context than their personal, emotional, or mental processes. Among the numerous publications this group produced is Paul Watzlawick's

The Situation is Hopeless, But Not Serious and *Insight May Cause Blindness, and Other Essays.*

These playful titles suggest the kind of approach that strategic family therapy developed. The systemic focus of this approach assumed that while families struggled with their problems, they also functioned according to the principle of homeostasis, in which they would resist change. Therefore, therapists had to be subversive regarding the problem so that the family would change inadvertently. One favoured intervention was the paradox. For example, the therapist would prescribe at the end of the session, "Between now and our next meeting, don't change anything." This could result in the family members paying attention to what shouldn't be changed, thus becoming attentive to possibilities for change. Strategic family therapy was brief, giving rise in time to solution-focused brief therapy developed by Steve de Shazer and his colleagues in Milwaukee. However, because of its subversive nature, it also attracted ethical attention because of the deception involved. For example, "prescribing the paradox" as an intervention worked because the family was not made aware of the assumptions that led to the prescription. The ethical principle of informed consent was breached in such a practice.

The Milan group – The Milan systemic model

Finally, there was a group of psychotherapists in Milan, Italy (the Milan Associates) who also had become frustrated with the psychoanalytic mode. The principal figures were Mara Selvini Palazzoli, Luigi Boscolo, Gianfranco Cecchin, and Guiliana Prata. Their significant contributions to the field of family therapy were the invariant prescription, positive connotation, and circular questioning. The *invariant prescription* was an instruction to parents to go out without telling anyone. This would serve to disrupt the family pattern and open the way towards healthier ways of relating. *Positive connotation* was the practice of describing a useful function for every symptom. For example, one member's depression might serve to keep the rest of the family connected. *Circular questioning* was a practice of asking questions that drew attention to the relational patterns and responsive sequences of behaviours among the family members. For example, "When you said that, what did she say? And what did you say then?"

Karl Tomm, family therapist in Calgary, published three articles in the late 1980s in the *Family Process* journal on the use of questions in therapy, their structure, and the intentions the therapists had in asking them. He recognized the influence of the Milan approach in the first of these articles.

D. Bowenian Family Therapy

One of the major contributors to the field of family therapy was Murray Bowen. What follows is a description of Bowen Family therapy theory and practice.

Murray Bowen's Career

Murray Bowen (1913-1990) began his career as a psychiatrist with an interest in schizophrenia, an interest shared by many practitioners and researchers of the era. His first place of work was the Menninger Clinic in the late 1940s where he observed the close relationship between schizophrenic patients and their mothers.

Bowen's interest in the field led him to the National Institute of Mental Health (NIMH) where he began to include whole families in his research. This involved admitting whole families to the hospital where they could be observed. Here he discovered that the emotional attachment between a patient and mother invariably involved the whole family. When this project ended in 1959, he moved to Georgetown University in Washington, DC, where he began working with a much broader range of families with less intense problems. He discovered that there are similarities of relational patterns among all families. These observations led him to develop what has become known as *Bowen Family Systems Therapy* which consists of eight "interlocking principles."

This work has been carried on principally at The Bowen Center for the Study of the Family. People who have carried this work forward include Betty Carter and Monica McGoldrick whose edited book, *The Family Life Cycle: A Framework for Family Therapy*, originally published in 1980 with a foreword by Murray Bowen, is a classic and has been reproduced as *The Expanding Family Life Cycle: Individual, Family, and Social Perspectives* (2015). Another practitioner is Michael Kerr who has written a very brief but useful description of the application of Bowen theory entitled *One Family's Story: A Primer on Bowen Theory*, (2004). A further application of these ideas is given in *Generation to Generation: Family Process in Church and Synagogue* by Edwin Friedman, first published in 1985.

Bowen's own publishing is preserved in a collection of essays entitled *Family Therapy in Practice* (1985). In chapter 21, he both outlines the eight principles and gives an account of his own journey of self-differentiation with respect to his family of origin. In one exchange, he notes how his mother began to write to him complaining about his father. He forwarded these letters on to his father, asking, "Did you know your wife was saying these things about you?" On a next visit, his mother said, "You read too much between the lines." To which he replied, "You write too much between the lines." This little exchange illustrates the process of detriangling in order to differentiate a self in one's family of origin.

The Eight Interlocking Principles

Murray Bowen loved theory. He was a great proponent of the maxim, "there is nothing as practical as a good theory." The eight interlocking principles demonstrate Bowen's belief that our work as counsellors must be guided by a rational theory. Theory is always present in the work of counselling, but counsellors are not always aware, in the drama of a counselling conversation, how they are being influenced by their theories. It's useful to reflect during and after session what role theory played in the way the counsellor interacts with the client.

Murray Bowen's eight interlocking principles are not only a useful way for students to think and reflect about family processes (including multigenerational processes), they are also useful for the student in reflecting on their own family of origin narratives, thus leading them to take steps towards their own self-differentiation—an essential part of the process in the development of the skills required for doing therapy.

Self-differentiation. The ideal that Bowen's theory presented is the idea of a differentiated self. By this, he means an autonomous individual, free from the family's emotional ego mass, and free of unresolved emotional attachments to one's family of origin. This does not mean that one is free of attachment, but of "unresolved" attachment. The goal of "resolving" emotional attachments is to be able to relate freely to other members of the family as equals.

This resolving assumes two forces, one that drives us to become emotionally separate, and the other that drives us to stay connected. Larry Crabb in *Understanding People* describes these two forces as the desire for belonging and mattering, or stated another way, security and significance. Thinking carefully about this two-pronged drive leads us also to reflect on attachment theory. We "attach" to our primary caregivers in the first months of life. The process of healthy development in those early years results in people who have a safe base from which they enjoy the freedom to explore their world. This is a description of a securely attached child, who will grow into a well-differentiated mature person.

An example of the application of these ideas is given by Lai & Bartle-Haring (2011) in an article entitled "Relationship among differentiation of self, relationship satisfaction, partner support and depression in patients with chronic lung disease." *JMFT, 37,* 2, 169-181.

> "The study serves to highlight the fact that the patient is part of a system, and that taking the system into account is relevant to the well-being of both the patient and the partner" (p.169).

> "Bowen defined differentiation of self at an individual level as the ability to balance two factors: (a) emotional and intellectual influences in cognitive functioning and (b) intimacy and autonomy in relationships. Differentiation at a system level refers to the system/family's ability to regulate itself. High levels of differentiation suggest that the family can make adjustments

when necessary and maintain a balance between separateness and connectedness. When this balance is not maintained, systems can become fused, without a sense of separateness among the individuals, or they can become cutoff and disengaged, without a sense of connectedness among its members. It is the balance of these two that allows individuals in a family to have a sense of belonging as well as a sense of individual identity that is supported by the family system (p.170).

The study goes on to discuss the helpful role of healthy differentiation within a family where a member has chronic lung disease. They found that "the partners' differentiation of self was ... a predictor of their relationship satisfaction ... (and) likely to be less emotionally reactive" (p.178) as they dealt with the additional challenges of a chronic disease. This example also demonstrates the wide applicability of systemic and relational thinking in working with people.

An idea like self-differentiation invites researchers to develop ways of measuring it. Bowen himself suggested that most of us were mid-range on a 1 – 100 scale. A very rigorous effort at producing an instrument to measure self-differentiation was conducted by Carolyn Licht and David Chabot (2006). Their literature review includes a description of previous efforts to produce a reliable instrument that could be used clinically. They hoped that the Chabot Emotional Differentiation Scale (CED) could be used both in assessment and in evaluating outcome of therapy. In the current post-modern climate in the field of psychotherapy, however, practitioners often prefer a more particular way of working with clients that considers their unique narratives rather than comparing them to some societal norm that scales such as the CED assume.

A biblical evaluation of self-differentiation is informed by the description of maturity given in Ephesians 4:14-15 where it states that, as we become mature, we attain to the "whole measure of the fullness of Christ" and become able to "speak the truth in love." We are then no longer infants "tossed back and forth by the waves" but become contributing members of a healthy community. This describes the maturity that comes with autonomy within a relationship.

An enlightening paragraph on differentiation is given by Stanley Grenz (2005) in his book-length evaluation of the theology of Wolfhart Pannenberg, specifically on his doctrine of the Trinity:

> "At the heart of Pannenberg's understanding of the doctrine (of the Trinity) are two important ideas. The first, self-differentiation, is traditionally used to refer to the bringing forth of the second and third trinitarian persons through the Father. So understood, it implicitly emphasizes the priority of the Father in the Trinity. Pannenberg, however, offers a radical reinterpretation of self-differentiation developed in the context of discussion of Hegel's understanding of personhood, namely, *that the essence of person lies in the act of giving oneself to one's counterpart and thereby gaining one's identity from the other.* His point is that the concept of dependence is bound up with personal self-differentiation. *The one who differentiates oneself from another is dependent on the other for one's identity.* This position builds from the thesis that person is a correlative term. Pannenberg finds this thesis in the entire Western tradition of the doctrine of the Trinity prior to Hegel, beginning with Augustine and including Richard of St. Victor and Duns Scotus, and he sees it as reminiscent of Maximus the Confessor, who taught *that unity and diversity do not exclude each other but*

increase proportionately. Yet for the substantial basis of this idea, Pannenberg looks to his analysis of the relationship of Jesus to the Father. (Grenz, 2005, p.48 emphases mine).

Other authors who present these ideas are Majerus and Sandage (2010). Their article discusses self-differentiation as a social science concept grounded in the Trinity and presents it as a construct for spiritual maturity. It is "being a relational self that can know one's own desires, feelings, and thoughts in the midst of being with, and giving themselves to, other people while maintaining boundaries" (p.43).

Triangulation: This discussion of differentiation sets the stage for the rest of the eight principles, beginning with triangulation. The basic concept here is that when stress between two people increases, a third becomes involved in some way in the relationship as a way to drain off the tension. The driving force of this development is anxiety. Rather than engage in the anxiety-laden one-on-one leveling conversation that a well-differentiated person could have, one of the partners speaks to a third, who is invited to see the issue from this partner's point of view. The triangled person then experiences some of that anxiety while the triangling person feels some relief since someone sees things from their point of view. In this sense, a relational triangle functions as structural triangles in architecture: it provides stability by lessening the anxiety experienced by one of the members of the triangle.

Bowen calls triangles "the 'molecule' of any emotional system" (1985, 469). Elsewhere, he states, "The triangle (is) a three-person emotional configuration, is the molecule of the basic building block of any emotional system, whether it is in the family or any other group" (p.373). "The best example is the father-mother-child triangle" (374).

In this example, a husband and wife differ on the degree of distance or closeness they want. This is influenced by their own attachment styles learned from their own families of origin. The partner wanting more closeness pursues the other, and the other withdraws. This creates some anxiety within each of them. This sets up the most common partner relationship pattern, pursue-withdraw, and often leads to conflict. It may also result in the partner wanting more closeness to turn to the oldest child to satisfy that desire. This child may then become involved in a relationship with the parent that becomes more than the usual parent-child relationship. On the other hand, the withdrawing partner may feel threatened by the demand for closeness and turn to their work or a hobby to avoid the anxiety-producing closeness.

While triangles provide stability to unstable dyadic relationships, they wreak havoc on intimacy. The family relies on triangles to help maintain an optimum level of closeness and distance between members while permitting them the greatest freedom from anxiety. The greater the fusion in the selves, i.e., the less the differentiation, the stronger will be the triangulation.

One of the challenges for the therapist is to learn to think in threes. Knowledge of triangles helps provide the theoretical perspective between individual therapy and family (systemic, relational) therapy. We can ask ourselves, whenever there is tension between two people, where is the third party? How might the third party be therapeutically included in the conversation?

The therapist's task in this work is to remain differentiated in the "heat" of the family's emotional system. It is easy to be drawn into the family's emotional "ego mass," and become triangled oneself. To prevent this, the therapist learns how to develop an alliance with the family as a unit rather than with one or another member, to develop an equal alliance with each member of the family, and to attend to the "here and now" of the emotional process in the room, rather than to get caught up in the content of their conflict.

The antidote to triangling is the development of level relationships between equals. The application of agape love, particularly as given in Ephesians 4, cited above, provides the biblical template for this. In v. 15, the word *truth* occurs as a verb; thus, we translate "truthing in love." This becomes possible as we develop our own self-differentiation by recognizing the anxiety that hinders it, discovering for ourselves that we are loved with a "perfect love that drives out fear" (1 John 4:18). We are then able to relate in a leveling way to others and our relationships are characterized with a love that can be described as "equal regard."

Nuclear Family Emotional System. Bowen theory suggests that we choose mates with levels of differentiation like our own. When differentiation is low, there is a high felt need for triangulation. Thus, two people with low differentiation marry and will triangulate a third person or other element in some way. Usually, one of 4 different symptoms will appear: a. physical or emotional dysfunction in a spouse: the other spouse over-compensates, and is often seen as a saint. b. overt, chronic unresolved marital conflict in which cycles of emotional distance and closeness occur. c. psychological impairment in a child. This enables the couple to focus on the child and ignore their own anxiety, the child absorbs the family anxiety, and the intensity of the parental relationship is diminished. d. emotional distance between the partners (Bowen, 1985, p.425).

One member of the family may become the "identified patient" (IP), the person with the problem. The family at a sub-aware level agrees that one member is the "problem." An individualistically oriented psychotherapy will agree with the family and seek to treat that person. Systemic, relational therapy, however, will understand the emotional process in the family and will see the whole family. The systemic phenomenon of homeostasis will mean that the family will seek to maintain things as they are. If the IP would really get better, it would mean that other parts of the system would need to change. For example, a disengaged father who becomes more engaged would result in the reduction of over-involvement of the mother. This would be a beneficial change for the whole family but would create some anxiety as the family members renegotiate the roles they each occupy in the family.

These unhappy results are due to the low level of self-differentiation of each partner. A biblical reflection on this includes the well-known verse often recited at weddings. "Therefore, a man shall leave his father and his mother and hold fast to his wife, and they shall become one flesh" (Gen. 2:24). The leaving referred to in this verse can be understood as an emotional self-differentiation from family of origin that makes possible the creation of a new family as the couple, both being well-differentiated, learn to build a new family together. At the stage of emerging adulthood when many people couple up, the self-differentiation process is not complete, and perhaps not even well started. The biblical solution for this is found in the teaching of mutual submission presented in Ephesians 5, the famous passage on marriage, in which one unfortunate but popular teaching is that the woman is to submit to her husband. The foundational concept there is the mutual submission presented in v. 21, "Submit to one another out of reverence for Christ." This mutual submission is possible because of the filling of the Spirit, (v. 18). This is an important part of the process of maturity described in Ephesians 4, referred to above. The bible does speak of authority in marriage. "For the wife does not have authority over her own body, but the husband does. Likewise, the husband does not have authority over his own body, but the wife does" (1 Corinthians 4:7). The mutual authority presented here is the counterpart to the mutual submission of Ephesians 5:21ff. Together these two concepts describe a relationship of equal partners of the kind envisioned in Genesis 1:27.

Family Projection Process: An example of this principle is when the most vulnerable child is triangulated into the parental relationship. Thus, the parents' own emotional fusion is "projected" onto this "chosen" child. This is especially problematic when the vulnerable child also has a legitimate need that requires extra care. The mother may become overprotective, the child may then respond by becoming demanding and more impaired, the father in turn becomes supportive in helping her deal with their problem child. With both parents focused on the care of the child, their own relationship may go untended as each allays their anxiety through extra care of the child.

A biblical reflection here may be the story of the nuclear family of Isaac and Rebekah, (Genesis 24 – 28). Each parent had their favourite child. The result was a severe enmity between the twins Esau and Jacob. A New Testament reflection on this is the parenting practices presented in Ephesians 6:4 – "Fathers, do not exasperate your children." One effect of a non-differentiated parent may be an "exasperating" way of relating to a child, which may involve either a too permissive or too authoritarian style. This is reiterated in Colossians 3:21 – "Fathers, do not embitter your children, or they may become discouraged." Parents who are well-differentiated will engage with their children in a way that will enable them to thrive.

The reader is encouraged to pursue the literature on parenting styles to gain a further understanding of the applicability of these verses.

Emotional cutoff: Emotional cutoff is another strategy that is used to manage anxiety within a system. Emotional cutoff can take several different forms from mild agreeing to disagree and thus never again addressing the subject to a total disengagement with one's family or one part of the family. There have been some family members who have not had contact with their family for many years. This strategy is not self-differentiation, because self-differentiation involves the maintenance of relationships. It is rather a strong reaction to the anxiety that is experienced in the family, sometimes experienced as hurt, but with a decision to sever the family relationship in some way. The severing can be geographical, as when a family member moves far away and cuts off contact. It can be psychological, as when certain topics become out of bounds for family conversation. Bowen (1985) stated, "An average family situation in our society today is one in which people maintain a distant and formal relationship with the families of origin, returning home for duty visits at infrequent intervals. The more a family maintains some kind of viable emotional contact with the past generations, the more orderly and asymptomatic the life process in both generations" (Bowen, 1985, p.383).

A biblical illustration of this phenomenon may be the story of the brothers Jacob and Esau, (Genesis 27: 41ff) in which Jacob flees from his brother in fear of his life after Jacob had cheated his older brother, at the behest of his mother, of the blessing rightly belonging to Esau. There is a resolution of the relationship between the two brothers when Jacob returns after a sojourn of several decades. However, the enmity between the descendants of the two men continues until this day in the ongoing conflicts in the Middle East.

Another may be the story of the prodigal son (Luke 15:11-32) where the younger of the two brothers asks for his share of the inheritance long before the father dies. It's interesting to speculate about the triangulated family emotional process between the two brothers and the father. The point of the story is the grace with which the father receives the lost son when he returns home. The celebration he throws raises a form of anxiety in the older brother who objects to the extravagance.

Multigenerational Transmission Process: Family projection process over several generations leads to severe dysfunction. For example, a couple with low differentiation projects on a certain child who is then more fused and less differentiated. This child marries one of a like level of differentiation, and they then project on one of their offspring, who then marries one of their same level of differentiation. Thus, the downward spiral continues over many generations.

Gunter, Riech and Almuth (2005) describe the understanding of this process as consisting of psychoanalytic theory of unconscious processes, systems theory, and the socio-historical dimension (p.129). The result is the perpetuation of family relational patterns over generations. For example, a husband and wife who have a withdrawing/pursuing pattern beget a son who repeats this pattern in his marriage. These patterns can be exacerbated by sociohistorical events such as wartime and economic depression. These authors believe that "severe psychiatric disorders always seem to result from traumata in the family system. Often these traumatizing events have taken place in the previous generation, who were not able to deal with them at the time" (p.135). They list severe illness, frequent deaths, loss of property or employment, forced migration, sexual abuse and others as examples of the kinds of trauma that may affect a family over generations. Larger communal catastrophes such as wildfires, wars and conflicts often bring their own trauma to families, individuals, and communities.

Readers are encouraged to explore their own family of origin stories in order to search out such nodal experiences. When I first began teaching in 1995, I instituted a family of origin assignment. The year 1995 is some 60 years removed from the Great Depression of the 1930s. Many of the family of origin stories included accounts of parents and grandparents surviving that period and developing relational patterns that enabled survival. Twenty-five years later those types of accounts began to disappear, but were replaced by students' stories of trauma, individual tragedies, and immigration.

The genealogies of the bible come to mind in this context. The first such genealogy is given in Genesis 5:1, "This is the written account of Adam's line." The book of Numbers begins with the genealogy of the Israelites. In the New Testament, both Matthew and Luke include a genealogy of the life of Jesus. Luke's version begins with Jesus and works all the way back to Adam, who is called the son of God (Luke 3). Luke thus emphasizes Jesus' membership in the human race. Matthew's account starts with Abraham. "A record of the genealogy of Jesus Christ the son of David, the son of Abraham (Matthew. 1:1). Matthew's emphasis is on Jesus' membership in the chosen people of Israel, and his place in the line of King David. An eye-catching detail in Matthew's account is v. 6, "David was the father of Solomon whose mother had been Uriah's wife." The NIV version softens this detail. The literal rendition is simply, "David begat Solomon of her of Uriah," indicating more precisely that she was Uriah's wife at the time of the tryst between David and Bathsheba. It's fascinating that a millennium after the event, this piece of sordid family history is considered important enough to be recounted. Yet it does invite further family systems speculation as well as important theological reflection about multigenerational transmission.

A more hopeful reflection on the multigenerational transmission process comes from the second of the ten commandments: "You shall not make for yourself an idol ... you shall not bow down to them or worship them, for I the Lord your God, am a jealous God, punishing the children for the sin of the fathers to the third and fourth generation of those who hate me, but showing love to a thousand generations of those who love me and keep my commandments" (Ex. 20:5). The "sin of the fathers" may include their sins and the ways they were sinned against. These effects filter down through the generation, but there is healing in the promise of love.

Sibling Position: This principle seeks to understand the interactive patterns between marital partners and the sibling position of each partner in his or her family of origin. This is the notion that birth order often predicts certain function within one's family emotional system. For example, the oldest child who marries a youngest will take responsibility which the youngest will expect the spouse to take.

A well-known book that discusses this phenomenon at length is Walter Toman's (1993) *Family Constellation: Its Effects on Personality and Social Behavior*. However, in most families, there are too many other variables at play that render this principle not very useful in the understanding of a family's processes. While the validity of the principle can make for interesting conversations—we have the over-functioning, oldest child, the overlooked middle, and the dependent youngest—it is easy to think of many examples that do not follow these expectations.

A biblical account that comes to mind is the story of Joseph and his brothers. Since there were four mothers, there were four oldest sons. Joseph was the youngest of the four oldest sons. As the father's favourite, he managed to incur the jealousy and wrath of his brothers, who eventually took action, selling him into slavery in Egypt. The roles of the other oldest brothers are not very obvious, except that Reuben, the oldest of all, lost his function as oldest brother to Judah, who became ancestor of the Jewish race. Joseph's role as an eldest became evident when as the prime minister of Egypt, he was able to save his entire family. The story has been popularized by the rock musical, "Joseph and the Amazing Technicolor Dreamcoat" by Tim Rice.

Societal emotional process: Bowen (1985) called this principle "societal regression" by which he meant that a society's emotional functioning can affect family emotional functioning. "In the 1960s, there was growing evidence that the emotional problem in society was similar to the emotional problem in the family" (p.386). The 1960s in western society were a time of considerable social upheaval. Bowen states further,

> "We are in a period of increasing chronic societal anxiety; that society responds to this with emotionally determined decisions to allay the anxiety of the moment; that this results in symptoms of dysfunction; that the efforts to relieve the symptoms result in more emotional band-aid legislation, which increased the problem; and that the cycle keeps repeating, just as the family goes through similar cycles to the states we call emotional illness" (p.386).

Unfortunately, this was the least fully developed of his eight principles. This is unfortunate because in the wake of the postmodern ideas of constructionism, our field has come to consider in more and more detail how the social discourses of our time influence the lives of people in their families, the social construction of the problems that people face, and how these social discourses become internalized in messages that re-enforce approved norms which may or may not be life-giving, and how the process of healing involves gaining freedom from conforming to the "patterns of this world" (Rom. 12:2).

In this principle, we may hear the call for justice that our work of counselling always entails. "What does the Lord require of you: To act justly and to love mercy and to walk humbly with your God" (Micah 6:8). "Seek justice, encourage the oppressed. Defend the cause of the fatherless, plead the case of the widow" (Isaiah 1:17). "For three sins of Israel, even for four, I will not turn back my wrath. They sell the righteous for silver, and the needy for a pair of sandals. They trample on the heads of the poor as upon the dust of the ground and deny justice to the oppressed" (Amos 2:6-7). Jesus proclaimed his manifesto in Luke 4, citing the prophet Isaiah: "The Spirit of the Lord is on me, because he has anointed me to preach good news to the poor. He has sent me to proclaim freedom for the prisoners and recovery of sight for the blind, to release the oppressed, to proclaim the year of the Lord's favor" (Luke 4:18-20). Indeed, Luke's gospel is a gospel of justice, specifically a lifting up of those who are oppressed. A narrow evangelical reading of this gospel might see the main oppression as being sin, and the remedy is faith in Christ for salvation. A detailed reading reveals his concern for the outsiders, those who have been othered, and by his attack on the oppressive religious system of the time. I believe that this eighth principle has far-reaching implications for us as we are involved in the work of helping people find freedom from the oppressive discourses which bind them.

Bowenian Goals of Therapy

The first goal of Bowenian family therapy is that adults must resolve their emotional attachments to their families of origin. "Resolve" is one of psychotherapeutic words that require definition. What does it mean to "resolve" an emotional attachment? Simply put, it means to gain greater freedom while maintaining a level relationship with others. Another term for it might be *the gaining of emotional intelligence.* As discussed in the section on differentiation above, it is the development of maturity. In this regard, Bowen has written a fascinating paper describing his own efforts to gain greater differentiation which he published in his book, *Family Therapy in Clinical Practice,* (pp.506ff).

The practical implication for family therapists is that they must achieve their own differentiation or they themselves risk being "sucked" into the emotional systems of the families they work with. To become the "non-anxious presence" that all therapists require to be, it is necessary to do this person-of-the-counsellor work. We need to take a voyage into our own families-of-origin in order to differentiate a self, to become aware of triangles and to de-triangulate, so that we can become "truthers in love."

The essential conditions for change include understanding—in order to separate thinking and emotion. Bowenian work involves the significant awareness of the emotional temperature in our emotional brain structures, engaging the prefrontal cortex in understanding, and developing more mature and less reactive responses. The purpose and process of therapy is to enable the client to "go home again," in order to arrive at a greater understanding of the another, in order to reduce the anxiety felt in the family of origin, so that those involved can relate freely as equals. One effective practice to achieve this is to collect family history stories, and then to reflect on them. Another is to inquire about others' memories of these stories, and of other members' experiences in their families. Even closely related siblings will have different experiences of growing up in the same family. In having these conversations, it is essential to listen with curiosity rather than to correct memories of specific details.

Practices of Bowenian Family Therapy

Bowen acknowledged his preference for theory and his impatience with technique. He outlined the following four steps in working with families.

1. Use genograms in order to learn about the family of origin, to discover its relational intergenerational patterns, its triangles, and the quality of relationships between the members of the family. Genograms are diagrams that illustrate a person's family members, how they are related, and their medical history. There are several good books on how to develop genograms, such as *Genograms: Assessment and Intervention, 3rd Edition* written by Monica McGoldrick, with Gerson, and Petry (2008). It is important to note here that the genogram is a tool for relating a family narrative, not for establishing an objective demonstration of the family's pathology. As a narrative, it enables specific conversations that highlight not only the problematic patterns but also the family steps to health.

2. Establish person-to-person relationships with as many family members as possible. We do this as therapists in our contact with each of the family members and by assisting the family

members towards this as well. Each family member will have a perspective of the family's narrative, and each must be honored. There may be push-back from some family members on details and meanings of an event, and the therapist needs to develop skills in "policing" conversations so that each member gets a fair turn. This will also have the effect of "normalizing" whatever experience different family members bring to the narrative.

3. Identify interpersonal triangles as the therapist participates in them. We may experience "pull" from one or more of the family members to see things from their point of view. As we attend to this pull, we are able to engage in conversation with the family member by the use of reflexive process questions that trace sequences of responses. This may lead to an enactment between two family members as they develop a more level relationship pattern between them.

4. Re-enter the family of origin. As we enter the family's "emotional ego mass," we begin to model a non-anxious interaction with each member, valuing the contribution of each member of the family. For adult members of the family, we may ask about the possibility of visiting in the case of a cutoff. We are able to raise anxious issues as necessary. As each family member hears the perspectives of each other member, their own perceptions of the problem and of the family change and they can more freely turn to each other in affirming ways. To facilitate this, the therapist takes an "I-position" in sharing their own perceptions, observations, and reactions. A woman who came to see me because of strained family relationships with her husband related how as a young child, she had been treated in special ways because

of a specific handicap she had. I wondered to myself if this had created some resentment on the part of the other family members. I coached her by wondering about visiting each other member of her family one by one, starting with the one easiest to talk to, and asking them what it was like for them growing up in their family. Week by week she came back to report on another visit. At the end of the process, she brought her husband to discuss their relationship. I believe that the relative freedom she attained with her family visits made it possible to look at her relationship with him in a healthier way.

Learning to Think Systemically

Bowen early identified a problem that all therapists in our culture will have. We have been squeezed into the individualistic mold of our culture. We think individualistically, as befits our culture. Further, the field of psychology has been primarily concerned with individual phenomena. Even though there has been development in social psychology and in interpersonal psychology, these approaches have mostly considered the individual's involvement.

We have the task of learning to think systemically and communally. Bowen describes the process he went through in learning to think systemically as three levels of awareness (Bowen, pp73f). The first, the intellectual level, is relatively easy. He understood that he had a family unit in the room, not just a collection of individuals.

The second level, the clinical, was to engage with the family as a unit rather than with each individual. One part of this was an awareness of the effect of the use of words such as diagnosis and patient, and the terms used to describe individual pathologies such as schizophrenia.

He describes this process as a change in the way he came to "know" the family. While he doesn't say this, I expect that thinking of the family in terms of the eight interlocking principles would effect a change towards this clinical awareness.

The third level is the emotional one. Here he identified three different emotional responses to the family. The first was to identify with one family member and blame the others. For example, a young therapist may hear a teen's story of parental strictness and decide that the parents need to be helped to loosen up the restrictions. The second emotional reaction was alternating over-involvement with each family member. When this young therapist hears the mother's account of the teen's abusive words, they decide that the teen needs some coaching in proper respect to parents. A more systemic practice would be to recognize the response-response pattern of the mother – teen relationship and to seek to bring change to that. The third emotional reaction was "a gradual detachment from stressful over-involvements and a beginning capacity to become aware of the overall family problem" (p.74).

Bowen's Family Systems Theory has been profoundly influential in the larger field of family therapy and indeed the whole field of psychotherapy and counselling. Terms like self-differentiation, triangling, and cutoff have entered the parlance of the field. The ideas of Bowenian theory provide a partial but important lens for hearing and interpreting the accounts that our clients bring to us.

CHAPTER 5

The Personal Aspect of Understanding Humans

In addition to considering the relational and systemic understanding of human behaviour and its application to therapy, we also need to have a clear concept of the individual's internal processes. This has generally been the stuff of psychology and is often referred to as psychodynamics.

As discussed earlier, the communal is theologically and socially prior to the individual. People Persons are birthed and raised by communities and are thus a product of communities. More specifically, persons belong to families, are raised by families, and continue the cultural traditions which produced them.

However, persons are also individuals, characterized by agency, responses, reactions, and interpretations of the experiences they encounter. Thus, it is necessary to look at who we are as such. In his book, *Understanding People*, Larry Crabb describes people as having four capacities: the personal, the rational, the volitional and the emotional. We will consider each of these in turn.

A. The Personal Capacity

The personal capacity describes most fully what it means to be an individual human being. Crabb states that all of us are motivated by two longings—our desire to belong and our desire to matter. We long to be part of a group, a community, an association, and within that belonging, we also long to matter. We seek both security and significance.

We encountered these ideas earlier in Chapter 4 when discussing Bowen's concept of self-differentiation, in which healthy self-differentiation is one in which we are able to relate well, as equals, to others. We want to be connected but also to be free to conduct our lives.

We also encounter these ideas in attachment theory, developed by John Bowlby and Mary Ainsworth (Nichols, 2017). Ainsworth developed the notion of attachment styles through her work with very young children. In her research, she observed the reactions of young children who were removed from their mothers for a short period of time. She observed how the children reacted when the mothers returned. She described three styles of attachment: secure, anxious, and avoidant. The secure attachment provided the child with a secure base from which to explore their world. They would greet the mother and then go off to play. The anxious child would run to the mother and cling. The avoidant child would perhaps not even acknowledge the mother.

Further research on parenting styles by Diana Baumrind (1969) suggested how these attachment styles on the part of children were the result of different parenting styles on the part of the parents.

She identified four possible combinations of parental authority and parental encouragement and found that the *authoritative* style of parenting, with a healthy balance of authority and love, was the most conducive to raising children with secure attachment styles. In contrast, *authoritarian* (emphasis on control), *permissive* (emphasis on love), and *neglectful* (providing insufficient levels of either) styles contributed to children who would display insecure attachment styles. Authoritarian parenting could lead to a withdrawing attachment style while permissive parenting could lead to anxious attachment style in children.

Sue Johnson (2008, 2013) described how these styles follow people into adulthood and affect their ways of relating as adults. These relational styles all stem from different ways of seeking to have our longings for security and significance satisfied in our most intimate relationships. According to authors Nichols and Davis (2017), speaking of Emotionally Focused Therapy for couples, state, "The therapist frames the couple's experiences in terms of deprivation, isolation, and loss of secure connectedness. This perspective, from attachment theory, helps family members focus on their longings rather than on each other's faults and failings" (p.143).

These different styles of attachment and complementary parenting styles all speak to how parental and social influences shape our experiences, and the individual's personal longing to belong and to matter, to have a place and to count, and for security and significance. From a creational point of view, we can say that this is what it means to be created as a person bearing the image of God. Both of these longings are reflected in Genesis 2, where we have supplementary content on the creation of humanity. The longing for significance is seen in "The Lord God took the man and put him in the Garden of Eden to work it and take care of it" (Genesis 2:15). The man was given work to do. We find significance in our work, which we deem as service, as a profession, as a vocation—language which speaks to our longing to matter. The longing for security is seen in Genesis 2:18, "It is not good for the man to be alone." The relational need is acknowledged and supplied in bringing another, like the man, to the man to be with him.

B. Rational Capacity

There are three ways in which we will discuss the rational capacity: Psychodynamically, from the perspective of attachment theory, and from a narrative point of view.

Psychodynamically: Crabb (2013) describes the rational capacity as consisting of two elements—images and beliefs. These consist of learnings about our world and our relationships in our world that begin very early in life. An *image* is a "relatively fixed representation of how things really are" (p.151). Our self-image concerns how we see ourselves. We have developed many terms for understanding the idea of self-image. We think about our self-worth, our self-esteem, and we have culturally defined notions of what healthy levels of self-esteem might be. Crabb insists, however, that there will always be some perceived deficit in our self-image. All human parents raise their children imperfectly, and the ideal of a fully securely attached child is just that, an ideal.

Our *beliefs* are our understanding of "how our worlds work and how we can function in our worlds in order to enjoy the satisfaction our hearts desire" (p.153). On the basis of our images and beliefs, we develop strategies that we hope will provide us the satisfaction of our longings for security and significance. For example, a non-athletic teen may become a scholar as a way of being recognized as having worth. A teen girl who isn't part of the "in-group" may develop friendships with a delinquent group of girls who are also not part of the in-group. As such teens grow into adulthood, their strategies may shift, but the underlying images and beliefs tend to remain intact without some intervention.

From **attachment theory**, we have the term *internal working models* (IWM) as a way of describing our internal life. IWMs are another way of thinking about who we are and how we engage with the world around us. In an article in JMFT, Keiley (2007) cites Bowlby (1969/1982) in describing these IWMs. Formed early in childhood, our IWMs consist of "beliefs and expectations about how attachment relationships operate and the possible gains and losses in these relationships. IWMs of the world include ideas of who the attachment figures are and how the attachment figures are likely to respond. IWMs of the self include ideas about how acceptable or unacceptable an individual is in the eyes of the attachment figures. Taken together, these IWMs of the world and self include information about what emotions are appropriate or possible for the individual to acknowledge and express and how these emotions help to maintain or deteriorate the attachment bond" (p.108f)

From a **narrative point of view,** we have the expression *narrative identity conclusions,* which refers to the stories we tell ourselves about ourselves. In my mind, this is a more holistic and integrated way of describing the phenomenon of one's self-image. The "narrative" indicates that we see ourselves in terms of the stories we have collected about ourselves. Sometimes, these stories are directed by our messages to our self. My feeling that I am stupid is supported by some event in my life that seems to support such a conclusion. "Stupid" is the conclusion of a story that I have remembered about that event. The story may include some feeling about that event, an embarrassment or shame or guilt. On the other hand, a happy event may result in a different kind of conclusion, one about my ability, or characteristic. The emphasis on this expression of "narrative identity conclusion" is that there is always a story that supports the conclusion. The advantage for therapy is that this story can be examined in a counselling conversation in order to discover exceptions to the conclusion. The conversation can look for other details in the story that have been obscured by the current narrative, thus providing for a more richly detailed account of the person. It is in my opinion a more effective approach to the healing of unhealthy identity conclusions than the direct confrontation which some other approaches imply.

The cognitive-behavioural perspective gives us the concept of "schemas," defined by Dattilio (2005) as "long-standing beliefs that people hold about others and their relationships. Schemas are a stable cognitive structure, not a fleeting inference or perception. They are differentiated from perceptions (attributions and expectancies) that a person makes from the events that he or she notices. Dealing with each family member's individual thoughts is central to cognitive-behaviour family therapy (CBFT). Although cognitive-behaviour theory does not suggest that cognitive processes cause all family behaviour, it does stress the concept that cognitive appraisal significantly influences family members' behaviour interactions and emotional responses to each other" (p.17). The beauty of Dattilio's definition is the way in which the author brings together the cognitive, the volitional and the emotional aspects of human experience in his description of "schema."

In this section on the rational capacity, we also need to consider the phenomenon of what has been called the "unconscious." One of my favourite exercises in class is to ask for a show of hands of all who believed they had an unconscious. Normally, everyone raised their hands. Then, I would ask, "How do you know?" This often resulted a deer-in-the-headlights looks from my students.

The idea of the unconscious has a history in psychology as long as the history of the modern scientific movement. An early contributor to this idea was Benedict Spinoza (1646-1673), who made a living as a lens grinder in Amsterdam, Holland, but made his contribution to the field of psychology in his work, *Ethics*, published posthumously (Watson,1968, p.163). Spinoza differentiated between conscious striving and unconscious desire. It is this notion that has led many to see him as the precursor to Sigmund Freud (p.164).

In his book, Watson (1968) provides a brief historical review of the idea of the unconscious from the Greek philosophers through the Middle Ages and up to the early modern era. Spinoza, and others that followed had some idea of the unconscious, but it was Freud that "grasped the crucial importance of unconscious motivation. It was he who found use for the unconscious, who thought that its exploration might help to explain otherwise inexplicable phenomena, and who saw that thoughts and feelings not in awareness played a role in directing behaviour" (p.459).

The notion of the unconscious has a long and controversial history in the field of psychotherapy. One of the most controversial aspects is the idea of the unconscious as the locus and repository of repressed memories. This became a phenomenon in the 1980s and into the 1990s as there was a recognition of the pervasiveness of sexual abuse and its effects. Several books on the theme of satanic ritual sexual abuse were published and it seemed as though an epidemic had been unearthed. Many therapists began to work with the practice of uncovering these repressed memories to help people heal from their abuse. Eventually, practitioners and researchers took a closer look at the phenomenon and the therapeutic practices associated with it and realized that some very unethical practices, such as suggestion, had crept into the work in this area. The phenomenon then inspired studies of memory and how they worked. A significant contribution to the debate was the book, *The Myth of the Repressed Memory*, by Elizabeth Loftus and Katherine Ketcham (1994). The authors discuss the history and effects of the practice of seeking to uncover repressed memories in light of their research in the "malleability of memory." The authors cite clinical psychologist Michael Yapko (1994): "Memory is a reconstructive process in which new details can be added to old images or old ideas, changing the quality of the memory" (p.266). They thus brought some sanity into this debate, and the "epidemic" has subsided significantly, aided no doubt by a few successful court cases against a few therapists. This history has also helped in amending the idea of the unconscious in the work of psychotherapy.

A common diagnosis that was related to the history of the unconscious was Multiple Personality Disorder (MPD). The theory was that parts of one's personality could be "split off." The more recent editions of the *Diagnostic and Statistical Manual of Mental Disorders* (DSM) have changed this to Dissociative Identity Disorder (DDI) which allows for a more nuanced understanding of this issue (pp.291ff). Yvonne Dolan (1991) writes that "Dissociation is more accurately viewed on a continuum, from ... daydreaming, spacing out ... traumatic amnesia and multiple personality" (p.140.) If this is so, all of us have dissociated. (My fear is that some readers might dissociate while reading this!) She further writes that "Healthy children dissociate when possible to protect themselves and survive experiences that they cannot otherwise control or escape (p.143.)

Larry Crabb (2013) has included the idea of the unconscious in his work. He uses the well-known metaphor of an iceberg. "Above the waterline are conscious behaviours, beliefs, and emotions. Below the waterline is a network of images and beliefs that we choose to hold but that we refuse to identify clearly. We direct our lives according to a set of ideas of which we remain largely unaware" (p.159). However, he also defines the unconscious in terms of awareness, a description of the unconscious that I much prefer. Much of the literature regarding the unconscious professes that we essentially have no control over its impulses and motivations without professional help. Much of what happens around us at all times is beyond our awareness as a matter of habit, and results in efficiency in living. If we had to attend to every impulse and stimulus, we wouldn't be able to get much done. However, memories can be recalled, the effects of our narrative identity conclusions on our actions and decisions can be brought to awareness and reconsidered, and we can grow in our awareness of these influences and practice ethical maturity in our lives. We grow "so that we may no longer be children, tossed to and fro by the waves and carried about by every wind of doctrine, by human cunning, by craftiness in deceitful schemes" (Ephesians 4:14).

Of course, at times it behooves us to attend to things that might have been beyond our attention. This process of searching the heart is enjoined in Psalm 4:4 (ESV) – "Be angry, and do not sin; ponder in your own hearts on your beds and be silent."

More recently, the findings of neuroscience and the involvement of the various structures of the brain has renewed an interest in the possibilities of unawareness. Daniel Goleman (1995) in his blockbuster *Emotional Intelligence* describes the involvement of two parts in particular, the limbic system comprised of the amygdala and the hippocampus, and the cortex—the first in charge of emotional response and the latter the part that thinks. Trauma studies have contributed a great deal to our understanding. There are indeed experiences that may become lodged in the emotional parts of the brain that bypass the thinking parts and can "trigger" responses that surprise us. Sometimes these are called flashbacks. The process of therapy generally then is to engage the thinking parts to accept and validate the traumatic experience with a view to living one's life with agency with respect to the traumatic experiences.

C. Volitional Capacity

We are agents in our lives who make choices and take actions. This fundamental idea of this capacity is described by Crabb (2013) as "The behavioral and relational strategies we engage to achieve security & significance." This definition fits very neatly with the model that he has constructed. First, in the personal capacity, our desire for security and significance motivates us; Secondly, in our rational capacity we develop a concept of who we are and how our world works. Thirdly, through our volitional capacity, we develop strategies congruent with that concept that we hope will achieve our desire for security and significance.

From an attachment theory lens, we might say that an anxious attachment is a strategy that may make us pursue ways we hope will satisfy our needs for security and significance. An avoidant attachment style may use distancing behaviours for the same reason.

This raises the question that psychologists have theorized and researched ever since there was psychology. Do we choose, or are we driven? Drive theories of personality and motivation have long been studied for their explanatory value regarding human behaviour. Many different drives have been postulated: drives for food, air, water, sex, companionship (Hebb, 1958, p.160). The impression left is that we are at the mercy of these drives, and that our behaviour will be determined to a large degree by our efforts to satisfy these needs.

A more elaborate development of this idea is Abraham Maslow's (1970) "hierarchy of needs," a concept that has had significant influence in popular psychology. In his classic *Motivation and Personality,* he developed a hierarchy of needs (illustrated with five levels of a pyramid) with physical needs forming the base and the pinnacle being the need for "self-actualization." The assumption was that lower-level needs had to be satisfied before higher level needs could be satisfied. There is a great appeal in this formulation: we certainly acknowledge that we have physical needs for survival, and other longings for fulfilment in our lives.

Building on Maslow's needs model, Kilpatrick and Holland (2006) state that "family problems encountered in helping situations can be clustered around various levels of need based on the primary need at that time" (p.3)—needs that include survival, self-actualization and spiritual needs.

There is certainly a place in our understanding of humans to think about these "needs." However, there is also a need to understand the effect of calling these "needs." Michael White in an entertaining video available on the Dulwich Centre website (dulwichcentre.com.au) asks, "How many of you have psychological needs? Would you raise you had if you have psychological needs? …. In western culture, people have had psychological needs since 1929. And they're increasingly popular; more and more people have psychological needs. This was a new understanding, that action is the surface manifestation of a psychological need; this is a relatively new idea in the history of the world's culture." His message is that words like needs, relationship dynamics, and internal resources construct our realities in certain ways that might be constructed otherwise if different language is used.

The central impact of this kind of construction of reality is the obscuring of human agency. The notions of drives, needs, etc., while they may have some use in our work in helping us to understand human behaviour, also have the side effect of obscuring the fact that we are also agents in our lives. Not only are we being acted upon by the society and culture in which we live, we are also responders who are making choices in our responses. The word "drive" connotes the idea of an irrational force beyond our control. In this section on volitional capacity, we want to explore what it means to be acting agents in our lives.

Addictions research may suggest otherwise, that there are forces within and beyond us that lead to actions that we cannot control. Gabor Mate (2018) presents the thesis that addictions are always a response to some psychological pain. He writes,

> "Such responses illuminate that addiction is neither a choice nor primarily a disease. It originates in a human being's desperate attempt to solve a problem: the problem of emotional pain, of overwhelming stress, of lost connection, of loss of control, of a

deep discomfort with the self. In short, it is a forlorn attempt to solve the problem of human pain. All drugs—and all behaviours of addiction, substance-dependent or not, whether to gambling, sex, the internet or cocaine—either soothe pain directly or distract from it. Hence my mantra: The first question is not 'Why the addiction?' but 'Why the pain?'"

In spite of the fact that the person with an addiction may feel helpless in the face of the addiction, the hopeful stance is still to believe that other responses to the pain are possible. A prime example of this is given by Viktor Frankl (1959). He writes of his experiences in the Auschwitz concentration camp in World War II,

"I may give the impression that the human being is completely and unavoidably influenced by his surroundings…. But what about human liberty? Is there no spiritual freedom in regard to behavior and reaction to any given surroundings? Is that theory true which would have us believe that man is no more than a product of many conditional and environmental factors – be they of a biological, psychological, or sociological nature? … We can answer these questions from experience as well as on principle. The experiences of camp life show that man does have a choice of action. There were enough examples, often of a heroic nature, which proved that apathy could be overcome, irritability suppressed. Man *can* (emphasis in the original) preserve a vestige of spiritual freedom, of independence of mind, even in such terrible conditions of psychic and physical stress. … everything can be taken from a man but one thing: the last of the human freedoms–to choose one's attitude in any given set of circumstances, to choose one's own way. And there were always choices to be made…." (Pp.103-104).

Frankl (1969) develops these ideas in his approach to therapy, which he has named *logotherapy*. He critiques Maslow's concept of self-actualization as being the highest need. He writes, "In my view, excessive concern with self-actualization may be traced to a frustration of the will to meaning. As the boomerang comes back to the hunter who has thrown it only if it has missed its target, man, too, returns to himself and is intent upon self-actualization only if he has missed his mission" (p.38).

The term that Frankl posits instead of self-actualization is self-transcendence. "Existence is not only intentional but also transcendent. Self-transcendence is the essence of existence" (p.50). As a person engages in a mission, they transcend themselves. "Man is pushed by drives. But he is pulled by values. He is always free to accept or to reject a value he is offered by a situation." (p.57). It is in this sense that the possibility of fulfilling the second great command, to love one's neighbour, becomes available to us. The value embedded in this command becomes the guiding light for us, founded in the response to the first, to love God with all one's strength.

The point to be re-emphasized here is that we are never simply passive recipients to stimuli to which we respond helplessly. The volitional capacity involves for us the ability to choose an attitude and an action. Thus, even doing nothing is seen as a response. We can ask the question, "How did you decide not to react?" Such a question often brings to light the volitional capacity and honours the agency of the person.

A systemic application of the volitional capacity is provided in the work of Karl Tomm and associates (2014). The authors have identified several different kinds of interpersonal patterns, some which move towards health, some which maintain a system, and some which move away from health. It is possible for family therapists to help the family member perceive their roles in the relational patterns by tracing out sequences of responses. "When he said that, what did you think? What did you do? And when you did that, how did you see this other family member respond?" As these patterns are traced out in the family conversations, agency comes into view, other options become visible, and space is opened for developing more healthy ways of interacting with one another. The relational strategies that Crabb posits, the intention of which is to satisfy our desires for security and significance can become transformed as we examine the values that pull us forward. The primary question for counsellors then is not what made you do that, but what were your intentions when you did that. As Alfred Adler pointed out, all behaviour is purposive. "Adler believed that **we are all born with a creative force**: the creative power of the individual. He did not reject the concepts of heredity, temperament, or disposition, but he emphasized that it is not so important what we are born with, but rather what we do with it" (Kelland, n.d.)

A more recent development of these ideas is seen in the reality therapy developed by William Glasser. His emphasis on volition, choosing and having intentions is seen in the titles of at least two of his books: *Choice Theory: A New Psychology of Personal Freedom* and *Counseling with Choice Theory: The New Reality Therapy*.

D. Emotional Capacity

Emotions can be understood as the positive or negative feedback that we receive that either reinforces the status quo or provokes us to change the strategies that we use to get our needs for security and significance met. We feel happy when these strategies work, and sad, disappointed, angry when they do not work, when our efforts to get our needs met are frustrated.'

Dattilio (2005) cited Lazarus (1991) who defined emotions as a "complex, patterned organismic reaction to how we think we are doing in life. Emotions express the intimate personal measuring of what is happening in our social lives. Therefore, emotions are integral to our close personal relationships."

Hebb (1958) linked emotion to motivation and stated, "Emotion is difficult to define precisely, or to use as a technical term." He saw the expression of emotion as the same as emotion. We believe, however, that a person is always experiencing some kind of emotion. It may be intense and visible, or low-key and unnoticeable. Our autonomic nervous system is always reporting something to us about the quality of what we are experiencing.

One description of emotion, as distinct from a definition, is that it is the combination of a physiological reaction and a contextual interpretation. For example, if I see a look of scorn on someone's face, I may feel shame. The observation of the look evoked an immediate interpretation on my part that that person was displeased with me and that I was lacking in some way, leading to the experience of shame. Since we are always involved physiologically in some way, we are always feeling some kind of emotion. Johnson (2013) writes that "emotion is actually nature's exquisitely efficient information-processing and signaling system, designed to rapidly reorganize behavior in the interests of survival" (p.66).

In this context, it is important to consider the emotional architecture of the brain and nervous system, the interplay of the emotional and rational centers, and the hormonal correlatives of those processes. Much has been written on this and I refer the reader to *The Body Keeps the Score* by Bessel van der Kolk (2014) and *The Anatomy of the Soul* by Curt Thompson (2010). For our purposes here, it is important to recognize two main structures in our brain, the limbic system consisting of the amygdala and the hippocampus, and the prefrontal cortex (PFC). The limbic system is the location of our emotional experiences, and the PFC is the location of our rational processes. Van der Kolk writes, "We depend on the amygdala to warn us of impending danger and to activate the body's stress response" (p.42). The PFC is the rational, thinking part of the brain. Its role is to evaluate the signals that the amygdala is receiving and sending. One of the problems with this system is that the amygdala and the PFC function at different rates, with the PFC reacting much more slowly than the amygdala. Van der Kolk cites neural research that discovered that when the amygdala is activated, for example, by a flashback of a trauma, an area of the PFC called Broca's area, went "offline" (p.43). This area is a speech centre in the brain, and this explains the neurological basis for becoming speechless in the face of a traumatic event. It is this neural structure and the process that it enables that leads us to fight, flight, or freeze. We are only able to stop and think after the fact.

One of the roles of counselling work is to re-story the traumatic experience in ways that engage the PFC so that it is able to take on its important work of regulating the limbic system. In a later section of his book, Van der Kolk writes about "befriending the emotional brain" (pp.206-219) in which he discusses the importance of observing the "interplay between thoughts and physical sensations" (p.209), the importance of a good support network—including a competent professional therapist who understands trauma and is able to engage the person in conversations that re-author the trauma stories in ways that make the possibility of life believable and attainable.

Western culture has developed an aversion to the consideration of emotions. Consider this unhelpful, but common, belief about emotions: "Live your life according to facts, not feelings." To which I reply, "Feelings are facts too!" In fact, feelings help us understand the facts that we are discovering or encountering. It is always legitimate to ask, "How do you feel about that?" (Which by the way is better than "How does that make you feel?" since it emphasizes that we have agency in respect to our feelings.)

Feelings have two generally useful functions. The first is the *barometric* function. Just as barometers measure the air pressure surrounding us, emotions give us a sense of the social or stressful pressure surrounding us. We may become aware of a tightness in our chest or a knot in our gut, or an underlying frustration. Or we may feel delight, or amusement. These are all signals that something is happening around us that is affecting us. These signals guide and motivate us to take action of some kind or other. Painful emotions will invite us to do something to avoid the pain. Happy emotions will motivate us to repeat whatever brought the happiness. All emotions lead us to the question, "What am I to do with this?

The second is the *existential* function. They are the signals that, in addition to motivating us to action, invite us to reflect on the meaning of life, on the values that we have given ourselves to, and the purposes and goals that have been our guiding principles. This function leads us to ask, "Why am I here?" and "What am I called to do?"

Thus, we will always respond somehow to our emotions, even if we haven't yet put a name to them. There are a couple of erroneous ways to respond. One is to ignore them, expressed in the idea that "I live my life by facts, not feelings." This usually means that the person is not aware of what they are experiencing, and the next step is an expression of anger on their part. Such persons are simply not aware of the signals that life is bringing them. Their belief is that attention to feelings simply distracts from reality.

The other extreme is to practice such an awareness of one's emotions that this becomes the most important aspect of life. The belief is that this is the way of authenticity. We are only really ourselves as we express ourselves. While there is a great benefit in awareness of what we are feeling, the practice of expressing our feelings does not by itself guarantee healing or change or growth. We get better at what we practice, and if we practice expressing our feelings, we will simply get better at that without necessarily achieving any growth in any of the ways that we hope to grow. Merely the *expression* of emotions is not a way to develop the "fruit of the Spirit" (Galatians 5:22-23).

The existential function of emotions involves reflection on the question of: *Why?* "Why do bad things happen to good people?" This question is considered by Rabbi Harold Kushner (1981) and a host of other theologians and philosophers. How can the existence of a good God, the existence of evil, and the idea of a powerful God all be true at the same time? The theological word for this discussion is "theodicy," the problem of a righteous God and the existence of evil.

Kushner's reply is that God is either not powerful, or that He has decided to limit His power.

Job's friends also sought to answer this question. When his three friends, Eliphaz, Bildad, and Zophar heard how he had lost everything, they came and sat with him for seven days in silence (Job 2:11-13). Their silence might have been the most helpful part of their visit! They spent the next twenty-nine chapters trying to convince Job that the reason for his suffering must be that he had sinned in some way and that God, in His justice, was punishing him for it. Job resolutely and steadfastly resisted their arguments.

Another answer to the "why" question is that God intends it for our growth. He is trying to teach us a lesson. The fourth of Job's friends, Elihu, takes up this argument after he realizes that the three older friends have been unable to convince or help Job and for the next five chapters seeks to convince Job of another way of thinking about what has happened to him. "God does all these things to a man—twice, even three times—to turn back his soul from the pit, that the light of life might shine on him" (Job 33:29-30). Essentially, he tells Job that there is a lesson to be learned in his sufferings if he will only attend to it.

Another effort to answer this painful question is the offer of the idea that "God is in control." This statement is often offered to people as an effort to bring comfort in the face of loss or suffering. A Calvinistic emphasis on the sovereignty of God requires this stance. I do not think it is a particularly comforting thought when one is in the depths of existential pain. The idea of God in control of all things does seem to have support in one way of understanding the final interlocutor with Job, God Himself. In the next four chapters of the book of Job, God describes his creative power and expression, and points out Job's smallness in comparison. Job's response to this is "repentance in dust and ashes" (42:5).

I submit that the first two of these three ways—suffering as a punishment for sin, and suffering as intended for our growth—are not helpful to people in suffering and are also not an accurate or useful way to answer the *why* question. The third answer, coming from the confrontation with God is better, especially when we consider the God revealed by Jesus' compassionate invitation, "Come to me, all who labor and are heavy laden, and I will give you rest. Take my yoke upon you, and learn from me, for I am gentle and lowly in heart, and you will find rest for your souls. For my yoke is easy, and my burden is light" (Matthew 11:28-30).

There is another way to understand God's discourse with Job, and that is simply to remind Job that whatever happens to him, his life is lived in the presence of the Creator, and in this context, he is accountable to his Creator for how he will live his life. Thus, his statement of repentance is not a turning away from sin or from some sinful act but is rather a coming back to where he started in the first chapter of the book of Job. After hearing of all his losses—wealth and family—he said, "Naked I came from my mother's womb and naked I will depart. The Lord gave and the Lord has taken away, may the name of the Lord be praised" (1:21). Rather than finding an answer to the *why* question, Job recognizes in the end, as he had at the beginning, that his life is lived in a posture of accountability to God, and thus turns to God amid his suffering.

It is also interesting to imagine the tone of voice when reading God's response to Job. I think mostly we hear a stern, scolding tone. How might God's words be heard differently if He spoke in a tone of compassion, reminding Job that He might look around and know that God is still God. "The God of the mountain is still God in the valley."

The existential question facing us in our suffering is the essential one, "How shall I respond to this? What is the faithful response as I find myself in this situation?" When people come to their counsellors with questions about why something has happened to them, counsellors can sit with—sometimes even in silence (as did Job's friends at the beginning of his misery) and find that their presence alone can be a source of comfort.

As it becomes appropriate, we can then engage in conversations about how they have responded, what has occurred to them as they have experienced and reflected on their experiences, and what that response bears witness to in their own character and humanness. As cited above, Frankl (1969) has stated that the final freedom each of us has is the freedom to choose our attitude towards that suffering. For us, it is the recognition that we continue to be in the presence of a God who, even as we walk through the valley of the shadow of death, continues to be our Shepherd (Psalm 23), a truth that has been radically emphasized in the gift of his Son who has claimed us as his own, and declared Himself to be the good Shepherd (John 10:1-18).

Certainly, the New Testament emphasizes the possibilities of personal growth in response to suffering. "God disciplines us for our good, that we may share in his holiness. No discipline seems pleasant at the time, but painful. Later on, however, it produces a harvest of righteousness and peace for those who have been trained by it" (Hebrews 12:11). "Consider it pure joy, my brothers, whenever you face trials of many kinds, because you know that the testing of your faith develops perseverance. Perseverance must finish its work so that you may be mature and complete, not lacking anything" (James 1:2-4).

Indeed, suffering is a feature of the ministry to which we are called. In Philippians 3, the Apostle Paul describes an attitude towards his life and his work in which he states that he has "lost all things" in order to "gain Christ and be found in him" (3:7-9). He caps this profound statement with an even greater profundity: "I want to know Christ and the power of his resurrection and the fellowship of sharing in his sufferings" (3:10). The highest privilege of ministry, of service, is expressed in this phrase: "the fellowship of suffering." For those called into the ministry of counselling and psychotherapy, this possibility of the fellowship of suffering becomes real each time we sit down with an individual, a couple, or a family. Our best work is done as we hear their story of suffering, and we empathize with them. Literally, as we empathize, we "suffer in" with them. We hear the painful story of loss or conflict or quandary, and as we listen, inwardly we resonate, in sorrow or anger or confusion. Sometimes this resonance has been called countertransference. In the work of counselling, countertransference is a reality and we must attend to it—but we must not allow it to turn us away from the fellowship of suffering, because it is in that fellowship, in which we weep with and rejoice with those who come to us, that, as this verse promises, we come to "know Christ."

There are three specific emotions that we will most often encounter in our meetings with those who come to consult with us. The first is the *sadness that comes with loss*. We are invited to these conversations to do what has come to be called *grief work*. This sadness can be extremely intense. One task of the counsellor is to hear, to accept, and to normalize accounts of the loss, and accounts of the reaction to the loss that we may hear. Sometimes, there have been efforts to soften the extent of grief, or to hinder its expression. It helps to be reminded of Jesus' own reaction to grief. In reaction to the death of his friend Lazarus, we have the shortest verse in the English bible. "Jesus wept" (John 11:35). In the Lazarus story, John uses two different words to describe Jesus' emotional reaction. *Embrimaomai* conveys the meaning of "deeply moved" and *tarasso* has the sense of being greatly troubled. Brown's *The Gospel According to John* (1966) translates Chapter 11:33 as "… when Jesus saw her also weeping, he shuddered, moved with the deepest emotion" (p.421). Brown explains this as the "emotional response prompted by the immanence of death …" (p.435). The two words together describe well the complexity of the emotional response when experiencing a great loss. In contemplating his own fate, he was "troubled in spirit" (John 13:21). The same word, *tarasso,* occurs here as Jesus contemplates his upcoming betrayal at the hands of Judas. These two instances that describe Jesus' own deep emotional reaction in the face of death, of both his friend's and his own, provide for us the biblical normalization of deep grief.

There has often been among Christian circles an effort to blunt the grief experience with verses about the assurance of heaven and the instruction to not let our hearts be troubled (John 14:1). These efforts have sometimes led people suffering loss to deny the depth of their emotions and evaluate them as evidence of the lack of faith or some other spiritual failing. It is far more helpful to help people with loss to recognize the value of what was lost as reflected in the grief that is felt. Grief is the evidence of love.

There are many resources that have been developed to help with this work. Perhaps the best known is GriefShare, a thirteen-session program with videos and discussion guides to help bereaved people grieve in company with others who have suffered a loss. It has been used widely in churches over the several decades in which it has been available. Another, developed by Dr. Bill Webster is "The Grief Journey," a collection of materials that aid in understanding and travelling the journey to which significant loss brings us. This material is available through Webster's website, https://griefjourney.com/.

The second emotion for our discussion in this section on emotions is *anger*. The English language has a rich vocabulary for expression degrees of this emotion. Annoyance, frustration, and irritation are just three of what could be a long list.

Anger has generally had a bad rap in western civilization, including in Christian circles. Two verses related to anger are Ephesians 4:27 – "In your anger do not sin': Do not let the sun go down while you are still angry," and Psalm 4:4 – "Be angry, and do not sin; ponder in your own hearts on your beds, and be silent" (Both ESV). In practice, both verses have often been read as injunctions to not be angry. Grammatically, however, both statements about anger are imperatives, as if we are commanded *to be* angry. The sense is the inevitability of anger in our lives and what to do about it. Psalm 4:4 suggests that anger is an invitation to introspection: we are to search our hearts and ask, what is this anger about for me? Ephesians 4:27 in context calls attention to the personal and relational effects of anger, situated as it is in the larger passage about growth to maturity that produces the ability to speak the truth in love.

In the circles of popular psychology, anger has come to have a reputation of authenticity. It is a mark of realness to be aware of our anger and what we are angry about. In his book, *Emotional Intelligence,* Daniel Goleman (1995) writes that "unlike sadness, anger is energizing, even exhilarating. Anger's seductive, persuasive power may in itself explain why some views about it are so common: that anger is uncontrollable, or that, at any rate, it *should not* (emphasis in original) be controlled, and that venting anger in 'catharsis' is all to the good." There are several popular approaches to psychotherapy that specialize in the expression of anger. I contend that such expressions may have a facilitative effect on the person, but as a therapeutic practice as an end in itself, it simply means that practicing cathartic expression of anger has the result that one gets good at it! More is needed, along the lines in the comments from Ephesians 4 and Psalm 4 above. Anger is an invitation to personal introspection: what does my anger say about me, my hopes, dreams and values? It is further an invitation to reflection on the relationships in which I am involved: how have I responded and been responded to, and how might I be motivated to improve these relationships?

A popular approach to helping people who have trouble controlling their anger is anger management. The basic approach in all of these strategies is the engagement of the thinking part of the brain in order to control the angry part—again, engage the PFC in order to control the outbursts of the amygdala. As one veteran of anger management courses said, they learned to tell themselves just before expressing anger, "I can if I want to. Do I want to?"

We understand anger to be a secondary emotion, one that follows a primary emotion. But because the amygdala is so reactive so quickly, the anger that shows up often obscures the primary emotion that we felt first. It is this phenomenon that Psalm 4:4 addresses. When we have recognized our anger, we need to take stock and seek to understand what it is that we felt first. The usual primary emotion is something like fear or hurt, but our natural wiring towards self-protection kicks in before we recognize this, and those close to us see the anger and not the underlying fear or hurt. Johnson (2008) has a lengthy discussion on this phenomenon in her work with couples based on Emotionally Focused Therapy for couples. Johnson describes her work with a couple by picking up on those words in their descriptions that are descriptive of the primary emotion, such as "agonizing" and "pushed aside" (p.132). These and others become clues to exploring the primary emotions which then lead to a different, softer, less defensive and more relationship-restoring conversation.

Therefore, we will experience anger, but growing emotional intelligence will enable us to manage it constructively and helpfully. Aristotle said, "Anyone can become angry—that is easy. But to be angry with the right person, to the right degree, at the right time, for the right purpose, and in the right way—that is not easy" (cited in Goleman, 1995).

A third common emotional experience is that of *depression and anxiety*. While these are two separate emotional experiences, they often occur together in human experience so we will treat them as such here. A pattern of circular thoughts beginning with a worry or anxiety about some event may lead to a sense of helplessness about the issue or event, and this helplessness results in a pessimistic view of the problem, generalized towards other aspects of life, and thus leading to depression. Many studies have been done on this phenomenon, seeking to understand the mental, emotional, physiological, and neurological processes involved. Many psychometric instruments have been developed in order to understand, measure, and treat these problems. While these will have some usefulness, the approach to counselling such people begins not with an assessment of the person's level of anxiety and depression, but with an attention to details of that person's life. What is the person's account of how anxiety and depression came to claim a place in their life? How has this problem affected the person's life, and in what ways has the person sought to stand up to this problem. Such a line of questioning will call forth memories, emotions, thoughts and actions that the person has felt, and may also lead to the discovery of ways of responding to and overcoming these feelings and living above them.

E. A 5ᵗʰ *Capacity: Social Capacity*

The fifth capacity, in addition to the four that Crabb (2013) describes (the personal, rational, volitional, and emotional) is the human ability and need to develop social relationships. Indeed, this need begins at conception, is embedded in the human experience at birth, and never goes away. The first four capacities all have their context and end goal in the social relationships and communities in which we find ourselves.

Human growth as persons has the *telos,* the goal, of maturity, shown in mature ways of relating, expressed in our thoughts, actions and feelings towards one another. The Greek word *telos* in its various forms denotes both an end goal, and the result of that end, maturity. Growth towards maturity is a process in which we not only have our own longings for belonging and mattering met in those relationships but can contribute to the meeting of those for the people around us. In fact, it is the ability to constructively engage in relationships so that the others sense their significance in the relationship while not having that reciprocated, that is one mark of maturity. Maturity like this is expressed in the Greek *agape* denotes a disinterested love, a love given for the sake of the other, without an interest in whether love comes back. Thus, loving God and loving the neighbour is completed by love of the enemy (Matthew 5:44).

In her book, *Peoplemaking*, Virginia Satir (1972) describes five different styles of communication that we engage in with others, including members of our own family. The first four are: placating in which we seek to placate another's unhappiness, blaming whereby we assign fault to another, computing in which we seek to maintain a superior, rational stance, and distracting whereby we seek to change the subject to something more comfortable. There is a fifth style that she calls *leveling* (p.72ff). Each of the others take either a one-down or a one-up stance towards another person in order to manage the tension in the relationship. Leveling, on the other hand, takes a "level ground" stance. It says in effect, "You are my equal and we can have a conversation about the issue."

This is what Daniel Goleman terms *emotional intelligence*, and what the Apostle Paul calls "maturity' as demonstrated in speaking the truth in love (Ephesians 4). It is also demonstrated in the descriptions that Jesus gave about the kind of human relationships that are characteristic of the kingdom of God (Matthew 5:20-48). He takes six sample rules and for each of them, he points to the human persons affected. "You have heard it said, you shall not murder" is the rule. "But I say to you" is the way he introduces the reason for the rule. There is a human person with whom you are dealing. Attend to the person, not just the rule. This is how your righteousness will exceed that of the scribes and the Pharisees (5:20). When we recognize that we are dealing with others like us, and related to them in leveling ways, and are able to truth in love, we attain something like the kind of maturity that God demonstrated in his own relationship with his people (5:48). It is person-centred rather than rule centred.

This kind of maturity is also described by the fruit of the Spirit as given in Galatians 5:22-23—"But the fruit of the Spirit is love, joy, peace, patience, kindness, goodness, faithfulness, gentleness and self-control. Against such things there is no law." It takes only a little thought to recognize that these nine characteristics are relational qualities, and that they are not abstract but rather evident in our relationships with others. These verses follow the "works of the flesh" (v.19) that includes a list of vices, including "fits of anger" (v.20). It is worth noting that the plural "works" is followed by the singular "fruit." The disintegration implied in "works" is countered by the integrity and maturity by the person who demonstrates life by the "fruit" of the Spirit.

CHAPTER 6

Narrative Therapy: Practices for Effective Relational Counselling

The previous chapters of this book have been devoted to a description of the ideas, theories and approaches to psychotherapy that provide a context and foundation for effective relational therapy. These ideas taken together form the basis of a body of knowledge and theory that are essential to an informed approach to this work. The goal of being able to be intuitively present with a client requires an educated intuition, and it is hoped that the ideas presented thus far will contribute to the realization of that goal. They give us the "what" of theory, the content of what we might think about when we are engaged in a helping conversation. They answer the questions about who people are, what problems are and how people change.

These ideas do not, however, give direct guidance on how a therapist is to engage in a conversation with someone who comes to them. They do not lead us in any direct way to understanding the "how" of therapy. The intention of this chapter is to provide that final step.

What is it that psychotherapists should *do*? How should they structure their questions? How should the counsellor engage with the person, couple or family coming to consult with them?

In this chapter, we will consider the recent so-called post-modern influences that have led to the development of narrative and other third-wave therapies, the practices that narrative therapists employ in their conversations, and the therapeutic stance that such counsellors take in their conversations.

A. Social Constructionism

We begin this chapter with a very brief discussion of the philosophical influences that produced what have come to be known as postmodern therapies. There are essentially three of them: *narrative therapy, solution-focused brief therapy*, and *collaborative languages* therapy. There are as many versions of these three as there are practitioners, but they all have in common the emphasis on how language shapes our realities. An example of this is the subtitle of the 1996 book, *Narrative Therapy: The Social Construction of Preferred Realities,* by Freedman and Combs. Language is a social function by means of which we connect with one another, and the words we use, and the narratives we tell with those words, construct our realities.

The word *reality* refers here to our experience of the circumstances of our existence as described to ourselves in words and narratives. It needs to be seen as distinct from what we usually mean by "objective truth" in that while we can affirm the existence of objective truth as an abstract principle, we can only know it as we describe it with our words based on our experience of the object which we are trying to describe. Ultimately, what we can know is limited to what we can describe. This means that it is also always open to revision.

Freedman and Combs have presented a fascinating example of this reasoning. They present four ideas that relate to this worldview. They are:

1. Realities are socially constructed.
2. Realities are constituted through language.
3. Realities are organized and maintained through narrative.
4. There are no essential truths" (p.22).

We consider each of these in turn. Our understanding of our experiences is put together, "constructed," in the context of the families, neighbourhoods, and communities in which we live. These understandings are described in the language that we share within those social contexts and are made understandable and meaningful through the ways in which they are woven through our stories into how we understand ourselves to be and exist within these communities. These understandings invite us then as counsellors to attend carefully to the words, the contexts of the words, and the narratives that those words convey, in our conversations with those who come to see us as the words and narratives constitute the "lived experience" of those who we counsel.

The fourth statement presents a conundrum, in that it exchanges the word *realities* for the word *truths*. There is certainly a trend among some social constructionists to say, or at least to tend to say, that since all we have is narrative descriptions of our realities, there is no objective truth to be known. This verges on the absurd. There are objects in our world which can be known with reasonable certainty.

How shall we then understand this fourth statement? One way is to rephrase the fourth statement by saying that there are only existential truths, that is, truths that are known only in our existing. Recall the discussion earlier in this book about the difference between epistemology and ontology. The first three statements above are epistemological affirmations in that they describe how we know things. The fourth switches to an ontological statement, about what is, or rather, what isn't.

It is manifestly obvious that there are some "hard" truths, such as the existence of the computer that I am using to write this book, and the desk upon which the computer rests A helpful discussion of this issue is provided by McGee, Del Vento and Bavelas (2005):

> "One point that the various approaches to social constructionism have in common is a recognition of the importance of discourse in constructing accounts of the social world around us. However, there are more extreme versions (e.g., Potter, 1996) and more moderate versions (e.g., Harré, 1983). We fall at the more moderate end, proposing simply that the presuppositions embedded in a question inevitably construct a version of events that could have been different. In particular, we have the greatest affinity for models that focus on the dialogue itself and the process of meaning co-construction by both participants. We do not agree with extreme versions of social constructionism that propose there is no reality, or that any version is as plausible as any other, or that words can mean anything that anyone wants them to mean, or that any perspective is as "good" (useful) as any other perspective" (p.372).

McGee et al (2005) simply affirm that narratives are constructed through the conversation processes that counsellor and client engage in. These narratives constitute our realities.

Another way of rephrasing the fourth statement might be to say that there are no un-storied truths. Every propositional statement that might be made about an object is made in a social context with the common language of that context and community. For example, the proposition "Jesus saves" can only be understood in the context of the story of Jesus, as that story is stewarded by the community that has formed around that story. It makes very little sense as an isolated, orphaned statement.

Daniel Taylor (1997) has written about the power of stories to shape our lives. Following is a collection of quotes from his book, *The Healing Power of Stories.*

- "But what ... is a story, anyway? Let me hazard a tentative definition, recognizing that most definitions leak. *A story is the telling of the significant actions of characters over time.*"
- "Here is one answer to the question of what we can know when we know a story. We can know we fit."
- "Stories not only give us ways of understanding reality, **they help determine what we are likely to perceive or be blind to—to recognize as real—**in the endless stream of data flowing around us that we call experience."
- "Stories, then, not only help us make sense of our present and past experience, they also allow us to imagine possibilities for ourselves in the future."
- "The power of the imagination links the past and present to the future, and gives us the possibility not only to know things, but to create whole new realities."

- "The great competitor with story as a way of knowing is reason, especially scientific reasoning."
- "Actually, even those of us most committed to logic and rationality do not so much reason our way to our views and values as *use* reason to justify what we find ourselves believing and valuing. And those beliefs and values are likely to have been formed by our stories."
- "Story provides us not only a way of knowing but also a way of remembering."
- "Without memory, knowledge is useless. It floats around as disembodied bits of observation and assertion, impotent and homeless."
- "Memory reminds us where any particular nugget of knowledge comes from, how it was discovered, how it has been used, where it has worked and where it hasn't. And the best medium for such memories is story."
- "We use memory of the past, our personal and collective past, to help us think and feel our way through the present. Remembering is the opposite of dismembering."
- "It is putting back together (re-member), or putting together for the first time, fragmented parts of past experience in a way that gives the past meaning for the present—and the result is story" (pp. 15-38).

In his award-winning 2001 novel, *Life of Pi,* Yann Martel concludes the story with the following dialogue, an interview with a news reporter.

"'We would like to know what really happened."

"Doesn't the telling of something always become a story?"

"Uhh ... perhaps in English. In Japanese, a story would have an element of *invention* in it. We don't want any invention. We want 'straight facts,' as you say in English."

"Isn't telling about something—using words, English or Japanese—already something of an invention? Isn't just looking upon this world already something of an invention?"

"Uhh ..."

"The world isn't just the way it is. It is how we understand it, no? And in understanding something, we bring something to it, no? Doesn't that make life a story?"

"I know what you want. You want a story that won't surprise you. That will confirm what you already know. That won't make you see higher or further or differently. You want a flat story. An immobile story. You want a dry, yeastless factuality" (pp.335-336).

The two authors cited here are both consummate storytellers and observers of the effect of stories as well as their ubiquity in our lives. Thus, we can see our work as therapists as being collaborators in the authoring of new stories in the lives of the people that come to us.

B. Narrative Therapy Practices

Narrative therapy can be described as a collaborative way of conducting oneself in helping conversations. The narrative therapist engages the client who has come to consult about some issue in their life. Narrative therapy is a set of practices based that attends specifically to the language that the client uses to describe their problem. It is the language and the narrative that the client brings that provide the grist for the questions that the therapist will ask.

The word *client* is used here since it is the most common word in the field of psychotherapy. It is problematic in its original meaning as it originally denotes one who leans on another. *Patient* refers to the medical model; *customer* suggests a commercial transaction; *persons who come to consult with us* is the preferred term for some narrative therapists. Each term presents something meaningful and has its own drawbacks. It is impossible to get away from at least some hierarchical understanding of the relationship, and thus we use the word *client* as the most common term in this field. The onus is still ethically on the counsellor to be accountable to the client for how the counsellor respects the autonomy and agency of the client and to be aware of the hierarchical status in the counselling work.

Michael White describes this ethical stance of accountability to the client as "decentred and influential." White (1997) writes that "In decentred practice, the knowledges and consciousness of the therapist … is not primary in providing a basis for a review of the real effects of the therapeutic conversation on the lives and the relationships of persons seeking consultation. Instead, it is the knowledge and consciousness of the client that is primary to, and privileged in, these considerations" (p.203).

In a brief, yet succinct, article published in a journal now incorporated into *The International Journal of Narrative Therapy and Community Work*, Erik Sween (1998) gives a "one minute" answer to the question, "what is narrative therapy?" Here is his answer, shortened to just a few seconds:

- The person is never the problem; the problem is the problem.
- The story is the basic unit of experience.

- Stories shape people's perspectives of their lives, histories, futures. Narrative therapy reshapes the stories.
- Stories sustain the meanings of the events of our lives. Narrative therapy enriches those meanings.
- Narrative therapy proposes that identity is created in relationships with others as well as by one's own history and culture.
- Of all the experiences that a person has had, some have more meaning than others. Narrative therapy focuses on building the plot which connects a person's life together.
- Our lives are crisscrossed by invisible story lines. Narrative therapy involves the process of drawing out and amplifying these story lines.

In the last book he published before his untimely death in 2008, Michael White wrote his definitive text on narrative therapy practices. He called the book *Maps of Narrative Therapy* (2007). In it he devotes a chapter to each of the following "maps" in the following order:

- Externalizing conversations
- Re-authoring conversations
- Re-membering conversations
- Definitional ceremonies
- Unique outcome conversations
- Scaffolding conversations.

He calls these "maps" and describes them as

"… constructions that can be referred to for guidance on our journeys—in this case, on our journeys with people who consult us about the predicaments and problems of their lives. Like other maps, they can be employed to assist us in finding our way to destinations that could not have been specified ahead of the journey, via routes that could not have been predetermined. … the maps presented in this book contribute to an awareness of the diversity of avenues that are available to preferred destinations" (p.5).

We discuss the following three first and then add the other three as addenda to the basic map. Three basic practices are externalizing, finding unique outcomes, and re-authoring.

Externalizing is the basic practice, indeed most often the starting point, of a conversation with a client. It is the practical application of the principle that the person is not the problem, the problem is the problem. In effect, it objectifies the problem and, in the process, personalizes the person. Zimmerman and Dickerson (1996) describe the problems that invade our lives as always attempting to take over our narrative identities, and the processes required to resist that capture. For example, "I am depressed" is an identity statement. The "am" indicates a totalizing kind of self-description that has come to pre-occupy the person at the expense of robbing of life and possibilities.

To externalize this problem, the adjective is grammatically changed to a noun and thus given an identity of its own. The therapist might reply with a question such as "When did depression first show up for you?" This question contains within it the assumption that there is a story related to depression, and that this story indicates some kind of boundaries around the problem which may allow for a greater freedom for life outside of those boundaries. Whereas "I am depressed" depicts a "thin" description of a life, the boundaries established by the question construct the possibility of a thick description as the edge and beyond is explored.

The biblical warrant for this exercise is found in Romans 7:16-17 – "Now if I do what I do not want, I agree with the law, that it is good. So now it is no longer I who do it, but sin that dwells within me." Here Paul draws a boundary between himself and sin and goes on to describe the victory that is in Christ. In essence, he externalizes sin as something other than he himself. The person is not the problem, the problem is the problem.

During the conversation, as the therapist includes externalizing language that objectifies the problem, the client will begin to adopt the same language and will come to be able to see the problem as something apart from who they are essentially. Clients come to see themselves as having a relationship with anger, anxiety, or sadness, rather than identifying with the problem. In the context of the relationship, they begin to see possibilities of agency that were not previously apparent.

The way this happens is in the search for **unique outcomes.** Unique outcomes are those details in a person's life that present as exceptions to the problem narrative. They are unpredictable from the perspective of the problem. Problems are very good at hiding these exceptions, obscuring them from notice, and generally discrediting them if they dare to show up in any perceptible way. This was evident in the story that one woman, whom we will call Evelyn, had of having been subjected to significant abuse as a young person and developing an interest in various crafts as a way of coping. The problem, "abuse," had discredited the enjoyment of crafts in such a way that her narrative was a very thin "I'm the victim of abuse and have found some coping skills by doing crafts." Another person, Micah, expressed guilt because of drinking too much in front of their family. "Guilt" brought the message of "you're a bad parent."

Unique outcomes become evident during these conversations about the objectified problem. There are two parallel pathways that such a conversation can take. The first is to map out the influence of the problem on the person. This will evoke accounts of the role that the problem has had in constraining the person's life, of limiting the family's range of relationship possibilities, of strictly controlling the perceptions that the partners in a couple relationship have of each other and their relationship.

During this part of the conversation, the counsellor listens for any indications of times when the problem has been less effective in its devious work, when for some reason it has not achieved its usual life-limiting results on the person. It is important for the counsellor to explore this first pathway in order to connect with the person, to seek to empathize with the plight the person finds himself in, and to give the person the experience of having been heard.

The second conversational pathway is to pick up on these exceptions and ask how it is that these became possible, and especially what the person did to contribute to this exception. The counsellor can also ask directly how the person has sought to stand up to the problem, what the person has done to lessen its power over the person.

These pathways become available to the counsellors as they commit to a certain value about who a human being, couple, or family is. Counsellors understand and commit to the conviction that the person is always more than the problem. Carl Rogers' (1951) famous maxim of unconditional positive regard comes to mind. Theologically, as bearers of the image of God, there is the awareness that the "echo" of that image can be heard in everyone if we take the time to listen. In Evelyn's story, referred to above, an hour-long conversation resulted in a very thick description of the various crafts in which she had been involved, and the excellence in them to which she devoted herself. The conversation included a discussion of her interest in ceramics, stained glass, petit point, and several other crafts. In some of these, her level of expertise was such that she offered classes in them for others. I was fortunate in that my wife had also been involved in some of these, so I had some working knowledge of what was involved. It became evident to me that this involvement in crafts was providing more than simply a way of coping. In Micah's story, I became interested in what it was about him that provided the ethical basis for the guilt. I understand that one feels guilty when one fails to live up to some value, or ethic or commitment, and I wondered how Micah might describe that value. It turned out that care for the children of the family, and providing a positive role model, was important to Micah.

In each of these situations, the "echo" is evident. For Evelyn, it consisted in the enjoyment of the crafts. For Micah, it was the value of positive parenting. Other therapists might have come up with other ways of describing these outcomes. This second pathway of inquiry, the effect of the person on the problem, is supported by the belief that no one is ever only a passive recipient of the events of life. We always respond somehow even when it seems we aren't in charge of our responses.

The third phase of a narrative conversation process is called *re-authoring*. This is the process of incorporating these unique outcomes into the person's narrative identity conclusion so that the thinly described "problem story" becomes thickened and textured by the inclusion of these unique outcomes so that the "narrative identity conclusion" includes all these other possibilities for the person. One way of illustrating this is as follows:

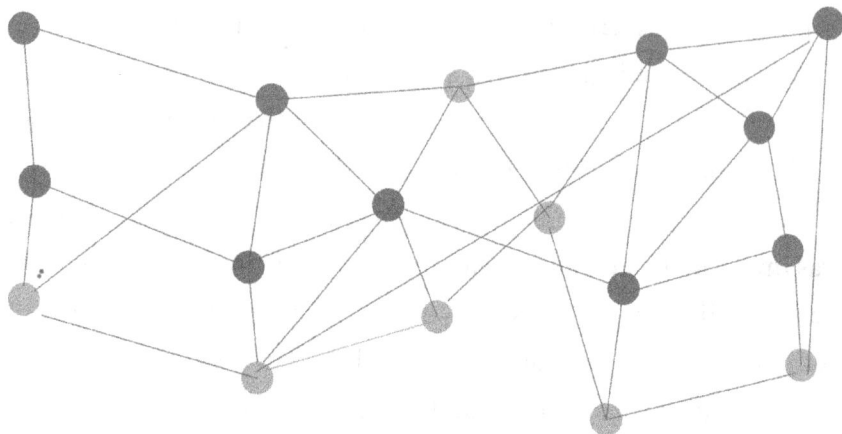

The red line connecting a single thread of dots represents a thinly described problem narrative, which includes only those parts of the person's life that correspond to the problem. The green line represents the results of a re-authoring conversation in which many of the other events of life—which had been discredited, or minimalized, or otherwise discounted by the problem—are rendered visible and meaningful. In Evelyn's account of her life, it occurred to me at the end of our conversation to ask, "Do you suppose, if you hadn't been abused, that you might still have been interested in crafts?" She paused a moment, and thought, and the expression on her face lit up, and she said, "Yes." Another pause, and then she said, "I do have a life!" In the conversation with Micah, I pursued a line of questions that explored his relationship with his children, his ideas and hopes for those relationships, the personalities of his children, and some of his joys about parenting. I asked towards the end of our first meeting, "What does it say about you, and who you are, that you hold such values in your life?" This led to some further discussion that resulted in overlaying the reason for the guilt with the commitment to the value especially as it related to parenting.

These three practices—externalizing, discovering unique outcomes, and re-authoring a narrative identity conclusion by incorporating the unique outcomes into the person's story line—constitute the basic practices of narrative therapy. In addition to these, as listed above, there are several other practices that have been developed as part of the process of re-authoring.

Scaffolding is a particular way of attending to the effect of questions that seeks to observe a person's readiness to learn new ways of understanding one's world and one's place in it. Michael White (2007) was influenced to think in this way by the work of Russian psychologist Lev Vygotzky (1986) whose interest was in early childhood education. Vygotsky's contribution to this work was the notion of "zone of proximal development" (White, 2007). The basic concept is the idea of what is possible to learn given what is already known. "This zone is the distance between what the child can know and achieve independently and what is possible for the child to know and achieve in collaboration with others" (p.271). Applied to narrative therapeutic practice, scaffolding is the practice of recognizing the distance between what a question assumes about the person's readiness for the question and the actual readiness for accepting the question. For example, the counsellor might ask, "What was that like?" This is an often-used open-ended question that invites the person to reflect on the experience being discussed. This question invites the client to ascribe some kind of meaning to the experience.

However, the client may not have reflected well enough to answer this. An intermediate question might be, "What did you do?" This would be more easily answerable, requiring only the client's recall. Subsequent questions such as, "What led you to do that?" "What happened then?" "What did you think?" "Why was this important to you to do what you did?" and a host of other such intermediate questions would fill in the gap between what happened and what that was like with an enriched account

An example of this is the story about Jenny who came to consult with me because of a stressful work situation, compounded by a difficult relationship with her husband. As we explored the effects of this problem on her and her response to the problem, she said, "I almost had an affair twice." This statement got my attention for several reasons. First, no doubt because of my sometimes-prurient interest in the sex lives of the people I meet with, but secondly, and more healthfully, and therapeutically, because of its ambiguity. I wondered to myself what she meant by "almost" and "twice" and how one almost does that twice. I asked Jenny, without clarifying any of those curiosities, "What stopped you?" She replied, "I'm not a piece of crap." I immediately recognized in her answer the echo of a value and life commitment that was important to her. I could have asked her then, "What does this say about you?" This could have led to a fruitful discussion along the lines of the re-authoring conversations described above. I thought though that it was a question that might be asking Jenny to make too big a conceptual jump. So, I engaged in a series of scaffolding questions that would bridge this gap. I asked, "What do you mean, "not a piece of crap?" She said something about how she valued fidelity in a marriage. I asked a follow-up series of questions along the following lines: "Why is fidelity important to you? How did that come to be important to you? How has that guided your life?" and finally, "What does this say about you?" This led to some fruitful descriptions of her narrative identity conclusions and affirmations about important values in her life.

A key feature of this practice is what is sometimes called "the difference that makes a difference." The main feature is that each question poses a difference that is approximately "just right" (to put a Goldilocks spin on it). If the gap is too big, it will seem impossible to jump, but if the question gap is too small, it will not matter or make a difference.

Another factor that the scaffolding conversations map has that makes it so effective is that it is a collaborative event. Jenny would likely not have come to put words to her narrative identity without the conversation that led to it. White states that the learning required for someone to traverse the zone of proximal development requires a conversational partnership.

This notion of the social context of learning is developed more fully in narrative work in the practices of **definitional ceremonies**. White (2007) describes definitional ceremonies as opportunities for "telling or performing the stories of their lives before an audience of carefully chosen outsider witnesses. These outsider witnesses respond to these stories with retellings that are shaped by a specific tradition of acknowledgment" (p.165). White and Epston (1990) attribute the idea of definitional ceremony to the work of Barbara Meyerhoff whom they quote: "I have called such performances "definitional ceremonies," understanding them to be collective self-definitions specifically intended to proclaim an interpretation to an audience not otherwise available" (p.191). The intent of these audiences is to provide an alternative community to the large one to which we all belong, an alternative that will honour a counter-narrative to the one that was supported by the constricting discourses of the larger culture. In other words, from the social construction idea that all of our understandings are held in the context of the communities and societies in which they make sense, there are some aspects of our societies and the metanarratives and cultural discourses that are constricting. These are included in the "rulers, ... the authorities, ... the cosmic powers over this present darkness, ... the spiritual forces of evil in the heavenly places" (Ephesians 6:12) to which we are not to be "conformed" (Romans 12:2).

The community of believers, the church, has served as a primary context in which counter-cultural stories could be told. Ideally, this community would be the locus for the definitional ceremonies of the kind that narrative practices describe. Unfortunately, the established, institutional church establishes its own schemas and discourses that sometimes need to be resisted as well.

The intent of the narrative practice of definitional ceremony is to create an audience that would hear the account of someone's experience with a problem, their resistance to the problem, and the ways in which they have reclaimed their lives from the problem. The definitional ceremony community is often described as made up of "outsider witnesses" who attend to the account and then report to this community, including the person relating the account, how the hearing of this story has affected them. The concluding step of such a ceremony would be for the original storyteller to relate to the outsider witnesses the effect that these tellings might have had on them. Within many Christian groups, there is a tradition of testifying which has many of the same characteristics of such definitional ceremonies. This tradition has often been powerful in its ability to strengthen participants' faith through these accounts.

A related practice in the field of therapy is what has come to be known as **reflecting teams.** The essential process is the same as described above in definitional ceremonies, where an audience is recruited to witness the telling of an account of a relationship between a problem and a person as that account develops during the therapy session. The main difference is that a definitional ceremony is an event that may culminate a series of therapy consultations to celebrate what has been accomplished by the person who came for the consultations. A reflecting team, on the other hand, could be present at every meeting and thus contribute to the therapy in a much more intimate, immediate and detailed way.

The practice of reflecting teams was introduced to the field by the Norwegian therapist, Tom Andersen (1987). A detailed description of the wide applicability of this practice is given in the book, *The Reflecting Team in Action,* edited by Steven Friedman (1995). The opening chapter by Tom Andersen is followed by chapters by practitioners who used reflecting team with families with violence, in schools, with "tough adolescents," in managed care, and many other contexts. A significant challenge of this practice is the human resource issue: where can one find persons to serve on the reflecting teams. This can become quite labour-intensive.

The final one of the six practices that White (2007) describes and that we will discuss is **re-membering conversations.** This practice also grows out of the influence of Barbara Meyerhoff on Michael White's practice. Meyerhoff was a cultural anthropologist who worked in a community of elderly Jewish people in Venice, a suburb of Los

Angeles. Many of these people were survivors of the Holocaust and had immigrated to the USA before or after World War II. They had understandably experienced significant loss, displacement, and disconnection. The result is often a diminishment of one's sense of identity as connections in a community with significant other people have been lost. This concept of self-identity runs counter to the modernist idea about how we each have a single self. This notion is addressed very fully by Charles Taylor (1992) in his *Sources of the Self*, in which he traces the history of the understandings of the self through the centuries of western civilization. In her work with this community, Meyerhoff was able to engage in community conversations that enabled the members of this community to reconnect with their personal and collective histories in ways that grounded them and gave a hope for their futures, not because of some kind of self-fulfillment but because of a grounding in community.

The postmodern, social constructionist stance understands that "identity is founded upon an 'association of life' rather than a core self" (White, 2007, p.129). Re-membering conversations then is not about "passive recollection but about purposive reengagements with the history of one's relationships with significant figures and with the identities of one's present life and projected future" (p.129). White quotes Meyerhoff: "To signify this special type of recollection, the term re-membering may be used, calling attention to the reaggregation of members, the figures who belong to one's life story, one's own prior selves, as well as significant others who are part of the story. Re-membering, then, is a purposive, significant unification, quite different from the passive, continuous fragmentary flickerings of images and feelings that accompany other activities in the normal flow of consciousness" (p.111).

Such conversations open up opportunities for people to acknowledge the contribution that others have made to their lives, and in turn, the contributions that they have made to the lives of others. As significant others are thus each re-membered into the person's "club of life" or "association of life," one's identity conclusions become enriched with thicker accounts of each of these relationships. These conversations are bi-directional, involving first an account of how the person being re-membered has contributed to the client's life, and then including an account of the contribution the client has made to the significant person's life. These accounts taken together contribute to an enlarged understanding of one's role in the community (club) and enhance one's own sense of the meaning and mattering of one's life.

This practice of re-membering was first developed in the context of grief and bereavement. This is of course not the only kind of loss we experience. There are many other kinds of losses that threaten our identities with insignificance and meaninglessness. Often these losses lead us to consult with therapists. These can include job losses, relocations, marriage breakups, relational estrangements, and many others traumatic events. Re-membering conversations can serve as a practice that can guide counsellors in their conversations with people who come with such accounts.

Therapeutic Stance

Narrative practices invite the counsellor to take a particular stance towards the client that is often at odds with the prevailing medical model, which consists of an expert assessment followed by a planned intervention. This follows the familiar diagnosis followed by a treatment. In contrast to this, narrative therapists adopt a not-knowing stance, one that begins with a practice of curiosity that is not guided simply by a hermeneutic based on presumptions derived from theories of problems and change. Rather, attention is paid to the language of the client and a curiosity about the possibilities of meaning that that language presents. While words have definite meanings and are used by clients with those meanings, there is always enough elasticity and ambiguity in any account that invites further questioning about those ambiguities, and the gaps in the stories. A curiosity that is not stymied by the presuppositions of theories, and not thwarted by unexpected answers, provides a way forward in any conversation. Such conversations are very much like Robert Frost's (1916) poem, *The Road Not Taken.*

> Two roads diverged in a yellow wood,
> And sorry I could not travel both
> And be one traveler, long I stood
> And looked down one as far as I could
> To where it bent in the undergrowth;
>
> Then took the other, as just as fair,
> And having perhaps the better claim,
> Because it was grassy and wanted wear;
> Though as for that the passing there
> Had worn them really about the same,
>
> And both that morning equally lay
> In leaves no step had trodden black.
> Oh, I kept the first for another day!
> Yet knowing how way leads on to way,
> I doubted if I should ever come back.

I shall be telling this with a sigh
Somewhere ages and ages hence:
Two roads diverged in a wood, and I—
I took the one less traveled by,
And that has made all the difference.

Every comment and every response the client makes is like a fork in the road and confronts the counsellor with a decision. Indeed, the options are often more than merely two! The counsellor responds to the client's response, having made a decision about what aspect of the client's response should be addressed by the next question. Very often, in pursuit of a unique outcome, or an exception to the problem, the response to the client's statement will indeed be the road "less travelled by" since the other problematic one has been worn with many passings.

Connected to this curiosity based on a stance of not-knowing, is the therapeutic stance of humility on the part of the counsellor. Curiosity is combined with a sense of wonder about the delightful complexity of the person, couple, or family sitting with the counsellor. We recognize that we will never get to the bottom of who it is that has come to see us, and that there is always more to learn. To put it in terms described earlier, we have the awesome opportunity to listen for the echo of the image of God in the individuals and the accounts of their lives that they bring to us.

A second feature of the therapeutic stance, that grows out of this listening for the echo of the image of God, is that we have put aside modernist notions of popular psychology that seeks to understand words and accounts as symptoms of internal, subconscious drives. Such ideas inform much of what has been termed as psychodynamic ways of understanding people. They trade in language about self-esteem, a "hierarchy of needs" and the like. Instead of this "internal drive" approach, the stance advocated for here commits to a search for "intentional states" (White, 2007, p.241). Intentional states instead inquire and seek to give voice and prominence to the commitments, values, beliefs, purposes, dreams, vision, and hopes that people have for their lives. Thus, someone who presents an account of an experience of guilt invites the counsellor to inquire about the moral standards that person holds to that they have failed to live up to. What does it say about them that they hold to such moral standards? A couple that comes with an account of conflict has a vision of a more harmonious marriage. How might that vision be made visible in a way that contributes to the achievement of greater harmony?

Someone might respond to this by asking, what if the person has no such moral standards? C. S. Lewis (2017) argues that there is such a thing as a "Law of Nature" in the old philosophical sense in which everyone knows that there is a right and wrong. There is much disagreement on what it is, certainly in specific instances, and among different cultures, and that people will quarrel about whether or not someone has breached the rules of right and wrong. But the fact that there is such a Law is a truth evident to all. The proof of it, he states, is in our creativity of the excuses we come up with when we do not live up to our own understanding of this Law. He states:

> "These, then, are the two points I wanted to make. First, that human beings, all over the earth, have this curious idea that they ought to behave in a certain way, and cannot really get rid of it. Secondly, that they do not in fact behave in that way. They know the Law of Nature; they break it. These two facts

are the foundation of all clear thinking about ourselves and the universe we live in" (p.7).

The point for our work is that it is possible, in our stance vis a vis the other, in our therapeutic conversations, to thicken the client's self-understanding in such a way that the values, commitments and moral standards become part of the narrative identity of the client. This is who I am, the person will come to believe, and it gives me strength. Thus, rather than seeing actions as indications of pathology, we see them as indications of purposes and commitments. Stories are the accounts of those actions, intentional states rather than internal states. Conversations about intentions give room for actions of personal agency, which make available for our clients the possibility of life-affirming responses to the problems that face them, which were not as evident when conversations revolve around depth of insight or other ways of seeking to understand oneself.

A Question of Metaphors

We conclude this chapter with a brief discussion about the various metaphors that often appear in conversations about therapy and counselling. There is, for example, the *depth metaphor*. This is the idea that it is essential for therapeutic conversations that they "go deep." Such depth is often displayed, it is believed, when deep emotions are expressed in session. As counsellors, we are always on the lookout for such emotions, whether tears, or anger or fear, and we have practices that serve to heighten those emotions so they can be resolved. When working in this metaphor, then, we seek to go beyond "surface" conversation, in which no deep emotions are expressed. This understanding of our work, however, has the effect of devaluing such surface talk, and often leads the therapist to overlook what may have appeared to be insignificant details in the client's account simply because they were not deep. In contrast to this, we want to value everything a client says as part of the content of our relationship with the client.

A related metaphor is "peeling the onion." This has the advantage of valuing the surface details since they have to be dealt with first in order to go deeper. Yet it still leads the counsellor to believe that the real work happens the deeper we go. So, counselling becomes the process of peeling the onion and crying with every layer!

Another metaphor of the like is the notion of needing to discover the *root cause*. The problem is understood to have a root cause that must be discovered before a solution can be applied to it. Again, this often has the effect of devaluing the content of conversations that one has along the road to that discovery. Practitioners of solution-focused brief therapy have taken a strong stance against this practice and have asserted that the solution doesn't need to have any relation to the problem, since therapy is not about understanding the problem, but about finding a way forward in life.

Sometimes clients come and tell us that they have "baggage" in their lives. Psychotherapy then becomes a matter of *unpacking baggage*. This metaphor is used in the title of a very helpful book by Jan and Don Frank entitled *Unclaimed baggage: Dealing with the Past on Your Way to a Stronger Marriage*. Many approaches to psychotherapy include a history, and such recounting in the course of therapy can be very important. They aid in helping the client feel heard, they provide accounts of interesting intergenerational patterns that invite one to reflect on one's current life, and they provide the grist for questions that will aid in discovering the unique outcomes that reveal the intentions that people have had as they have lived their lives. The risk that comes with the baggage metaphor is that counselling then becomes simply unpacking baggage and displaying all the dirty laundry that has been packed away. This can bring with it the effect of becoming stuck in a problem-saturated account of a life or relationship without having discovered any way forward. It may have the counterproductive effect of explaining why a person is where they are without necessarily providing a map to go forward.

In contrast to this is the *narrative landscape* metaphor. When painting a landscape, the artist attends to each detail as an essential part of the overall picture. Every detail adds to the overall impression and experience the landscape leaves with the viewer. It is the same in our conversations with our clients. Every word matters, and we lend significance to those words as we hear them, wonder about them, and ask further questions about them. White (2007) describes a "landscape of identity" that develops as a result of a "trafficking of stories about our own and each other's lives" (p.80). The outcome of such "trafficking" is the construction of our narrative identities. In our conversations with the people that come to consult with us, we make inquiries that lead to descriptions of actions (landscapes of action) and to descriptions of meaning (landscapes of meaning) as the clients reflect on the significance of the actions. Such reflections are the result of questions that we ask as we maintain a stance of curiosity and humility in these conversations. These landscapes emerge as we engage in the various practices of narrative therapy described above.

Three baseball umpires were discussing their philosophy on calling balls and strikes. The first said, "I calls 'em as they is." The second said, "I calls 'em as I sees 'em." The third said, "They ain't nothin' till I calls 'em." The landscape metaphor is more like the approach of the third umpire, except that the counsellor doesn't have the centred position of authority that an umpire does. It would fundamentally change the baseball game if each pitch's quality was the result of a negotiation between the umpire, the batter, the pitcher, and likely also the manager. In our counselling work, however, the metaphor applies. An action is ambiguous until it is storied, that is, until its location in the context of the life of the person or family is described in a meaningful way.

It is essential that we examine the metaphors that are implicit in our understanding of our work. These metaphors guide us in what we attribute significance to in our therapeutic conversations, and they might lead us to deem as insignificant, or to even overlook details in our clients' accounts of their lives that do not fit our metaphor. Thus, we are not cooks peeling onions, we are not baggage handlers unpacking dirty laundry, and we are not root pickers digging up root causes. We are landscape artists, attending to the many details and their locations in the narratives that shape the possible meanings that each detail of a person's life may have.

Conclusion

Someone asked me once, "How can you sit there all day and listen to those sad stories."

The question startled me. I realized that I had never thought of my work as a counsellor in that way. My second thought was, "That's not what I do. I hear a lot of stories of courage."

One of my guiding bible verses for this work and for my life is Philippians 3:10. In the context, Paul writes about all his achievements as a scholar and Pharisee. "If anyone else thinks he has reason for confidence in the flesh, I have more: circumcised on the eighth day of the people of Israel, of the tribe of Benjamin, a Hebrew of Hebrews; as to the law, a Pharisee; as to zeal, a persecutor of the church; as to righteousness under the law, blameless" (Philippians 3:4-6). He then disclaims them and lists them as liabilities rather than assets. "I count them as rubbish" (3:8) is the ESV's rendition of a word that more colorfully and more literally could be translated as a certain barnyard material. Instead, he states as his life goal these words: "I want to know Christ and the power of his resurrection and the fellowship of his suffering."

I have come to see how this verse describes succinctly and accurately how the ministry of counselling fulfills our calling. Every client brings a story of some narrative of some kind of relational disquiet. As we enter with them into the counselling relationship and empathically hear their stories, we indeed enter the "fellowship of suffering." In this way then we actually get to "know Christ." On the one hand, we become the presence of Christ as we have followed Jesus into this work, and to this particular client. And then we hear the other side of the story, from when Jesus said, "Truly, I say to you, as you did it to one of the least of these my brothers, you did it to me." Here is where we recognize the sacredness of our work: Jesus comes to us in the people we have the privilege of serving! We experience the "fellowship of suffering." It is in that fellowship that the narrative is re-authored, that the disquiet is healed.

In this light, it behooves us as Christian counsellors to first seek the sincerest self-knowledge so that we bring to this work the emotional maturity and the spiritual sensitivity that it requires, and secondly, that we continue to be students of this work, developing the practices that enable us to stay current with the latest developments in our field of service.

If you have read this far, let me remind you that this book is a bit of a primer, an introduction to, and a very brief review of what I believe are some basic ideas required to be an effective counsellor. These are the things that should be known. Beyond this comes the task of learning the art of counselling. We learn to counsel by counselling and then, with the help of skilled supervisors and colleagues, reflect on how we have done it.

Along with the knowing and the doing comes the experience, the emotional involvement in which we engage as we give ourselves to the work. Our personal awareness of our own inner life as we are listening and engaging with the people who come to us becomes the ground on which we then reflect on what we have done—asked and answered—in the counselling conversation. Then we reflect on how what we have done is guided by, adds to, or contrasts to the theory we have brought into the conversation. We are engaged then in a recursive process involving our own knowing, doing, and feeling.

This process is described by James Olthuis as "the beautiful risk." It is risky, in that we enter into an unpredictable collaboration with our clients rather than into a controlled conversation. "We need to let pain be pain in order to listen to its message" (Olthuis, 2001, p.182). But it's beautiful because we encounter the other as a person of equal value whom we accept with equal regard, that is, agape love. "There is a flow from the personal to the interpersonal and to the cosmic, back and forth, from I to we, from we to creation, from creation to God. Finding our home in God's redeeming and forgiving love, we are increasingly able to let be and flow with the processes of life without needing to control them—without any guarantee except our faith in the God of love" (Olthuis, p.223).

This all happens in the context of the dialogue with the other. And it is in that fellowship of suffering that we become aware, while engaged with the other, of the Other, the one in whose Name we serve.

References

Introduction

Tomm, K. (1987a). "Interventive interviewing: Part 1. Strategizing as a fourth guideline for a therapist." *Family Process* 26 13-31

Tomm, K. (1987b). "Interventive interviewing: Part 11. Reflexive questioning as a means to enable healing." *Family Process* 26 167-183

Tomm, K. (1988). "Interventive interviewing: Part 111. Intending to ask lineal, circular strategic and reflexive questions." *Family Process* 27 1-15

Chapter 1

Adams, J. (1970). *Competent to Counsel*. Nutley, NJ: Presbyterian and Reformed Publishing Co.

Augsburger, D. (1986). *Pastoral counseling across cultures*. Philadelphia, PA: The Westminster Press

Benner, D. G. (1988). *Psychotherapy and the Spiritual Quest*. Grand Rapids, MI: Baker Book House

Bulkley, E. (1993). *Why Christians Can't Trust Psychology*. Eugene, OR: Harvest House

Clebsch, W. A. and Jaekle, C. R. (1964). *Pastoral care in Historical Perspective*. New York: J. Aronson.

Clinebell, H. (1966). *Basic Types of Pastoral Care and Counseling*. Nashville, TN: Abingdon Press. Updated and revised by Bridget Clare McKeever (2011).

Gregory the Great. (nd). *The Book of the Pastoral Rule of Saint Gregory*

Collins, G. (1980). *Christian Counseling: A comprehensive guide*. Waco, TX: Word Books.

Collins, G. R. (2000). An integration view. In Johnson, E. L., and Jones, S. L. *Psychology and Christianity: Four Views*. Downers Grove, IL: InterVarsity Press.

Crabb, L. (1977). *Effective Biblical Counseling*. Grand Rapids, MI: Zondervan Publishing House

Crabb, L. (1987). *Understanding people: Why we long for relationship*. Grand Rapids, MI: Zondervan

Haley, J. (1996). *Learning and teaching therapy*. New York, NY: Guildford Press

Hauerwas, S. (2022). Being with the wounded: Pastoral care within the life of the church. ABC Religion & Ethics. https://www.abc.net.au/religion/wounded-pastoral-care-within-the-life-of-the-church/10708802.

McMinn, M. R. and Campbell, C. D. (2017). *Integrative psychotherapy: Toward a comprehensive Christian approach*. Downers Grove, IL: IVP Academic

Nichols, M. and Schwarz, R., *Family Therapy: Concepts and Methods, 7th Edition*. London, UK: Pearson.

Nichols, M. and Davis, S., *Family Therapy: Concepts and Methods, 12th edition*. London, UK: Pearson.

Powlinson, D. (2010). *The biblical counseling movement: History and context*. Greenboro, NC: New Growth Press

Soldan, W. (2018). "What I need for orientation" *Christian Psychology Around the World*, 11, 40-47

Kitzingen, Ger. European Movement for Christian Anthropology, Psychology, and Psychotherapy (EMCAPP)

Tomm, K. (1987a). "Interventive interviewing: Part 1. Strategizing as a fourth guideline for a therapist." *Family Process* 26 13-31

Tomm, K. (1987b). "Interventive interviewing: Part 11. Reflexive questioning as a means to enable healing." *Family Process* 26 167-183

Tomm, K. (1988). "Interventive interviewing: Part 111. Intending to ask lineal, circular strategic and reflexive questions." *Family Process* 27 1-15

Chapter 2

Adams, J. (1970). *Competent to Counsel*. Nutley, NJ: Presbyterian and Reformed Publishing Co.

Bartle-Haring, S., Bryant, A., and Whiting, R. (2022). Therapists' confidence in their theory of change and outcomes. *Journal of Marital and Family Therapy*, 48, 4, 1190-1205.

Beck, J. R. and Demerest, B. (2005). *The human person in theology and psychology: a biblical anthropology for the twenty-first century*. Grand Rapids, MI: Kregel.

Collins, G. R. (2000). An integration view. In Johnson, E. L., and Jones, S. L. *Psychology and Christianity: Four Views.* Downers Grove, IL: InterVarsity Press.

Crabb, L. (2013). *Understanding people: Why we long for relationship.* Grand Rapids, MI: Zondervan.

Farnsworth, K. E., (1985). *Wholehearted Integration: Harmonizing Psychology and Christianity through Word and Deed,* Grand Rapids, MI: Baker Book House.

Hunsinger, D. van D. (1995). *Theology and pastoral counseling: A new interdisciplinary approach. Grand Rapids,* MI: Eerdmans.

Johnson, E. L. (2010). *Psychology and Christianity: Five Views.* Downers Grove, IL: InterVarsity Press.

Nichols, M. and Schwartz, R. C. (2006). *Family Therapy: Concepts and methods, sixth edition.* Routledge

Sherlock, C. (1997). *The doctrine of humanity.* Charles Sherlock. Downers Grove, IL: InterVarsity Press.

Skinner, B. F. (1962). *Walden Two.*

Chapter 3

Barker, M. J. and Iantaffi, A., (2019) *Life isn't binary: On being both, beyond and in-between.* London, UK: Jessica Kingsley Publishers.

Berg, I. K. and de Shazer, S. (1997). *No more lectures [videorecording (VHS)] : building solutions with a family in crisis : a consultation interview,* Milwaukee, WI: Solution Focused Brief Therapy Centre.

Berg, S. (2015). Can Christians do Narrative Therapy? Original Goodness instead of Original Sin as the Starting Point for

Therapy and Theology. *The EMCAPP Journal: Christian psychology around the world,* number 7.

Berg, S. T. (2020). *Significant Strides in Soul Spotting,* http://growmercy. org/. Posted on May 24, 2020

Brunner, E. (1952). The Christian doctrine of creation and redemption: *Dogmatics,* Vol. II. Philadelphia, PA. The Westminster Press.

DeFranza, M. K. (2015) *Sex difference in Christian theology: Male, female, and intersex in the image of God.* Grand Rapids, MI: Eerdmans.

Daschuk, J. (2013) *Clearing the plains: disease, politics of starvation, and the loss of Aboriginal life.* Regina, SK: University of Regina Press.

Derrick, J. M. (2017). *Kahwà:tsire: Indigenous Families in A Family Therapy Practice With The Indigenous Worldview As The Foundation.* Unpublished dissertation.

Dueck, A. (1995). *Between Jerusalem and Athens: Ethical perspectives on culture, religion, and psychotherapy.* Eugene, OR: Wipf and Stock.

Dueck, A. and Byron, K. (2011) Community, spiritual traditions, and disasters in collective societies. *Journal of psychology and theology, 39,* 3, 244-253.

Fowers, B. J. and Davidov, B. J. (2006). The virtue of multiculturalism: Personal transformation, character, and openness to the other. *American psychologist, 61,* 581-594.

Frankl, V. (1969). *The will to meaning: Foundations and applications of logotherapy.* New York, NY: New American Library.

Grenz, S. (1997). *Sexual ethics: An evangelical perspective.* Louisville, KY: Westminster John Knox Press.

Haley, J. (1996). *Learning and teaching therapy.* New York: Guilford Press

Holland, J. (2006) *A brief history of misogyny: The world's oldest prejudice.* London, UK: Constable & Robinson, Ltd.

Hollinger, D. P. (2009). The Meaning of Sex: Christian Ethics and the Moral Life. Grand Rapids, MI: Baker Academic

Hook, J. N., Davis, D. E., Owen, J., Worthington, E. L., and Utsey, S. O. (2013). Cultural humility: Measuring openness to culturally diverse clients. *Journal of counseling psychology, 60,* 353-366.

Hook, J. N. and Davis, D. E. (2019) Cultural humility: Introduction to the special issue. *Journal of psychology and theology, 47,* 2, 71-75

Inman, A. G., Mesa, M. M., Browne, A.L., and Hargrove, B.K. (2004). Student-faculty perceptions of multicultural training in accredited Marriage and Family Therapy programs in relations to students' self-reported competence. *Journal of Marital & Family Therapy, 30,*3, 373-388.

Manteufel, A. (2005). *Chromosomen non est omen* – on the relationship between neurobiology and psychotherapy. *Journal of Systemic Therapies, 24,* 3, 70-88.

Niebuhr, H. R. (1951). *Christ and culture.* New York; Harper & Row, Publishers.

Pinnock, C. (1996). *Flame of Love: A theology of the Holy Spirit.* Downers Grove: InterVarsity Press.

Seikkula, J., Karvonen, A., Kykyri, V.-L., Penttonen, M. and Nyman-Salonen, P. (2018). The Relational Mind in Couple Therapy: A Bateson-Inspired View of Human Life as an Embodied Stream. *Family Process, 57:*855–866.

Sherlock, C. (1997). *The doctrine of humanity.* Downers Grove, IL InterVarsity Press.

Smith, M. S. (2019). *The Genesis of Good and Evil The Fall(out) and Original Sin in the Bible.* Louisville, KY: John Knox The Westminster Press.

Stern, D. (2007). Applying developmental and neuroscience findings on other-centred participation to the process of change in psychotherapy. In S. Braten (Ed.), *On being moved. From mirror neurons to empathy* (pp.35–47). Amsterdam, the Netherlands: John Benjamins Publishing Company. https://doi.org/10.1075/aicr

Taniguchi, N. (2005). From polarization to pluralization: The Japanese sense of self and Bowen theory. In *Voices of Color: First person accounts of ethnic minority therapists.* Rastogi, Mudita & Wieling, Elizabeth, Eds., 263-276. Thousand Oaks, CA: Sage Publications Inc.

Toews, J. E. (2013). *The story of original sin.* Eugene, OR: Pickwick Publications.

Younjou Seo, (2010). Outcomes assessment, Briercrest graduation requirement.

Chapter 4

Bateson, G. (1972). *Steps to an ecology of mind.* Chicago, I: The University of Chicago Press. Bateson, M. C. (2000) Foreword.

Bland, E. D., and Yoo, C. (2022). Clinical integration and thirdness: A discussion of difference, supervision, and power. *Journal of Psychology and Christianity, 42,* 3, 238-250

Boszormenyi-Nagy, I., and Sparks, G. M. (1973). *Invisible Loyalties: Reciprocity in intergenerational family therapy.* Hagerstown, MD: Harper & Row, Publishers.

Bowen, M. (1985). *Family therapy in clinical practice*. Lanham, MD: Rowman and Littlefield Publishers, Inc.

Carter, E. A. and McGoldrick, M. (1980). The family life cycle: A framework for family therapy. New York: Garder Press, Inc.

Grenz, S. J. (2005). *Reason for Hope: The Systematic Theology of Wolfhart Pannenberg, 2nd edition*. Grand Rapids, MI: Wm. E. Eerdmans Publishing Co.

Kerr, M. (2004). *One Family's Story: A Primer on Bowen Theory*. Washington: Bowen Center for the Study of Family. Available at https://www.thebowencenter.org/publications-products

Lai, A., and Bartle-Haring, S. (2011). Relationship among differentiation of self, relationship satisfaction, partner support and depression in patients with chronic lung disease. *Journal of Marital and Family Therapy, 37*, 2, 169-181

Licht, C. and Chabot, D. (2006). The Chabot Emotional Differentiation Scale: A theoretically and psychometrically sound instrument for measuring Bowen's instrapsychic aspect of differentiation. *Journal of Marital & Family Therapy, 32*, 2, 167-180.

Majerus, B. D., and Sandage, S. J. (2010). Differentiation of self and Christian spiritual maturity: Social science and theological integration. *Journal of Psychology and Theology, 38*, 1, 41-51.

McGoldrick, M., Gerson, R., and Petry, S. (2008). *Genograms: Assessment and Intervention, Third Edition*. New York: W. W. Norton.

McGoldrick, M., Preto, N. G., and Carter, E. A. (2021). *The Expanding Family Life Cycle: Individual, Family, and Social Perspectives*.

Minuchin, S. et al (1967). *Families of the slums; an exploration of their structure and treatment*. New York: Basic Books.

Mittleman, B. (1944). Complementary neurotic reactions in intimate relationships. *Psychoanalytic Quarterly, 17:* 182-197

Napier, A. Y. and Whitaker, C. (1978). *The family crucible: The intense experience of family therapy.* New York: Harper & Row, publishers.

Nichols, M. P. (2010). *Family Therapy: Concepts and Methods, 11th Edition,* Boston: Pearson.

Nichols, M. P. and Davis, S.D. (2017). *Family Therapy: Concepts and Methods, 11th Edition,* Boston: Pearson.

Ray, W. A. and Nardone, G. eds. (2009). *Paul Watzlawick: Insight may cause Blindness and other essays.* Phoenix, AZ: Zeig, Tucker and Theisen.

Richmond, M. E. (1917). *Social diagnosis.* New York: Russell Sage.

Satir, V. (1972). *Peoplemaking.* Palo Alto, CA: Science and Behavior Books, Inc.

Satir, V. (1983). *Conjoint family therapy, third edition.* Palo Alto, CA: Science and Behavior Books, Inc.

Seegobin, W. (2023). Racial Healing in the Church: The Usefulness of the Interpersonal Process in Therapy Model. *Journal of Psychology and Christianity, 42,* 2, 116-126).

Toman, W. (1993). *Family Constellation: Its effects on personality and social behavior.* New York: Springer

Tomm, K., St. George, S., Wulff, D. and Strong, T., eds. (2014). *Patterns in interpersonal interactions: Inviting relational understandings for therapeutic change.* New York: Routledge.

Whitaker, C. (2011) Work with family: From an experimental session of Re-Empowering the family. https://www.youtube.com/watch?v=1O83anXmvv8. Retrieved Jan. 30, 2023

Yalom, I. D. (2020). *The theory and practice of group psychotherapy, sixth edition.* New York

Chapter 5

American Psychiatric Association (2013). *Diagnostic and Statistical Manual*

Baumrind, D. (1971). Current patterns of parental authority. *Developmental psychology monograph, 4,* 1, Part 2, 1-103.

Bowlby, J. (1969/1982). *Attachment and loss.* Vol. 1: Attachment. New York: Basic Books.

Brown, R. E. (1966). *The gospel according to John,* (i-xii). Garden City, NY: Doubleday & Company, Inc.

Crabb, L. J. (2013). *Understanding People.* Grand Rapids: Zondervan.

Dattilio, F. (2005). The restructuring of family schemas: A cognitive-behavioral perspective. *JMFT, 31,* 1, 15-30.

Dolan, Y. (1991). *Resolving Sexual Abuse.* New York: Norton.

Frankl, V. (1959). *Man's search for meaning: An introduction to logotherapy.* New York: Simon and Schuster.

Frankl, V. (1969). *The will to meaning: Foundations and applications of logotherapy.* New York: New American Library.

Glasser, W. (1998). *Choice Theory: A new psychology of personal freedom.* New York: HarperCollins.

Glasser, W. (2000). *Counseling with choice theory: The new reality therapy.* New York: HarperCollins.

Goleman, D. (1995). *Emotional intelligence.* New York: Bantam Books.

Hebb, D. O. (1958). *A textbook of psychology.* Philadelphia, PA: W. B. Saunders Company.

Johnson, S. (2008). *Hold me tight: seven conversations for a lifetime of love.* New York: Little, Brown and Company.

Johnson, S. (2013). *Love sense: The revolutionary new science of romantic relationships.* New York: Little, Brown and Company.

Keiley, M. K. (2007). Multiple-family group intervention for incarcerated clients and their families: A pilot project. *JMFT, 33,* 1, 108.

Kilpatrick, A. C. and Holland, T. P. (2006). *Working with families: An integrative model by level of need, fourth edition.* Boston: Allyn and Bacon.

Kelland, M. (n.d.) *Adler's individual psychology.* https:// socialsci.libretexts.org/Bookshelves/Psychology/ Culture_and_Community/Personality_Theory_in_a_ Cultural_Context_(Kelland)/04%3A_Alfred_Adler_and_ Harry_Stack_Sullivan/4.03%3A_Adler's_Individual_ Psychology#:~:text=Adler%20believed%20that%20we%20 are,Adler%2C%201932a%2F1964).

Kushner, H. S. (1981). *When bad things happen to good people.* New York: Anchor Books.

Lazarus, R. S. (1991). *Emotions and adaptation.* New York: Oxford University Press.

Loftus, E. and Ketcham, K. (1994). *The myth of the repressed memory.* New York: St. Martin's Press.

Maslow, A. (1970). *Motivation and personality.* New York: Harper & Row.

Mate, G. (2018). *In the realm of hungry ghosts: Close encounters with addiction, Revised edition.* Toronto, ON: Vintage Canada.

Nichols, M. P. and Davis, S. D. (2017). *Family therapy: Concepts and methods, 11th edition.* Hoboken, NJ: Pearson.

Satir, V. (1972). *Peoplemaking.* Palo Alto, CA: Science and Behavior Books, Inc.

Thompson, C. (2010). *The anatomy of the soul: surprising connections between neuroscience and spiritual practices that can transform your life and relationships.* Carol Stream, IL: Tyndale House Publishers.

Tomm, K., St. George, S., Wulff, D. and Strong, T., eds. (2014). *Patterns in interpersonal interactions: Inviting relational understandings for therapeutic change.* New York: Routledge.

Van der Kolk, B. (2014). *The body keeps the score: Brain, mind, and body in the healing of trauma.* New York: Viking

Watson, R. J. (1968). The great psychologists: From Aristotle to Freud, second edition. Philadelphia, PA: J. B. Lippincott Company.

White, M. https://dulwichcentre.com.au/michael-white-archive/michael-white-video-archive/

Yapko, M. (1994). *Suggestions of abuse: True and false memories of childhood sexual trauma.* New York: Simon and Schuster.

Chapter 6

Andersen, T. (1987). The reflecting team: Dialogue and meta-dialogue in clinical work. *Family Process, 26,* 415-428.

Frank, J. and Frank, D. (2003). *Unclaimed baggage: Dealing with the past on your way to a stronger marriage.* Colorado Springs, CO: NavPress.

Freedman, J. and Combs, G. (1996). *Narrative therapy: The social construction of preferred realities.* New York: W. W. Norton and Company.

Friedman, S. editor. (1995). *The reflecting team in action: Collaborative practice in family therapy.* New York: The Guildford Press.

Frost, R. (1915). The road not taken. *Atlantic Monthly,* August.

Harré, R. (1983). *Personal being: A theory for individual psychology.* Oxford: Blackwell.

Lewis, C. S. (2017). *Mere Christianity: The Case for Christianity, Christian Behaviour & Beyond Personality: A Classic of Christian Apologetics and One of the Most Influential Books amongst Evangelicals.* Musaicum Books. Kindle Edition.

Martel, Y. (2001). *Life of Pi.* Toronto, ON: Vintage Canada.

McGee, D., Del Vento, A. and Bavelas, J. B. (2005). An interactional model of questions as therapeutic interventions. *Journal of Marital and Family Therapy, 31,* 371-384.

Meyerhoff, B. (1982). Life history among the elderly: Performance, visibility, and re-membering. In J. Ruby (Ed.), The anthropology of experience (pp.261-286). Chicago: University of Illinois Press.

Potter, J. (1996). *Representing reality: Discourse, rhetoric and social construction.* London: Sage.

Rogers, C. (1951). *Client-Centered Therapy: Its current practice, implications, and theory.* Boston: Houghton Mifflin.

Sween, E. (1998). The One-minute Question: What Is Narrative Therapy? *Gecko, Vol. 2,* 3-6.

Taylor, C. (1992). *Sources of the self: The making of the modern identity.* Cambridge, UK: Cambridge University Press.

Taylor, D. (1996). *The Healing Power of Stories: Creating Yourself Through the Stories of Your Life.* New York: Doubleday.

Vygotsky, L. (1986). *Thought and language.* Cambridge, MA: MIT Press.

White, M. (1997). *Narratives of therapists' lives.* Adelaide, Australia: Dulwich Centre Publications.

White, M. (2007). *Maps of narrative therapy.* New York: W. W. Norton and Company.

White, M. and Epston, D. (1990). *Narrative means to therapeutic ends.* New York, NY: W. W. Norton and Company.

Zimmerman, J. L. and Dickerson, V. C. (1996). *If problems talked: Narrative therapy in action.* New York, NY: The Guildford Press.

Conclusion

Olthuis, J. (2001). *The beautiful risk.* Grand Rapids, MI: Zondervan.

Acknowledgements

This book is the result of many significant influences in my life. Here are some who deserve recognition for the contributions they have made, with sincere apologies to those who also deserve to be mentioned but that I've failed to remember.

I am grateful to the faculty of the Eastern Baptist Theological Seminary (now Palmer Seminary) of Philadelphia for their innovative program in Ministry to Marriage and Family where I was introduced to the burgeoning field of family therapy, its pioneers, and its theories. This learning significantly enriched my pastoral ministry. Special thanks go to Myron Chartier, Peter and Carol Schreck, and David Augsburger. Then, I need to thank the faculty of the Briercrest College and Seminary who decided to take a chance on me, a between-jobs pastor, and offered me a teaching faculty role. Paul Magnus and Dwayne Uglem were the people that interviewed me on that fateful weekend in July 1995. I don't know if I said anything that impressed them, but at least I guess I didn't hurt my chances, since they offered me the job. I am also grateful for the significant financial and moral support they provided through the resources of Briercrest Seminary as I pursued professional status as a Clinical Fellow and Approved Supervisor with the American Association for Marriage and Family and the Canadian Registry of Marriage and Family Therapists.

There are some significant friendships that I formed through the years. I need to acknowledge Samuel Raj who has been a stimulating conversation partner, and colleagues in the Saskatchewan Branch of the Canadian Association for Marriage and Family Therapy. Specifically, George Enns, Jan Shadick, Dennis Arbuthnot, Ryan Melin and others as we pioneered our profession in our province. Thank you for your collegiality!

I need to mention the many students whom I have had the privilege of having in my classrooms. Your questions, comments, disagreements, and challenges were stimulating and served to sharpen my work. "Iron sharpens iron" certainly applies to the classroom. I wish I could name all of you here.

I'm so grateful to the people who have now taken up the torch in carrying the counselling programs at Briercrest forward. Margaret Clarke and Carley Pagens were both students during the time I taught. The program is now under the very capable hands of Margaret, with significant assistance from Carley.

I've saved the most important mention to last. Erika has simply been the rock who has been my touchstone throughout my professional and personal journey. Her day-by-day support and those turning-point conversations have come together to shape me and our life together. I have acknowledged the voice of God in my life and how often that voice has sounded like you! Thank you, thank you!

Finally, I acknowledge that I am Jesus-follower. I am grateful for the "abundant life" which he has promised (John 1:10). It has truly been such.

About the Author

Sam Berg is a native of Saskatchewan, Canada. He has an undergraduate degree in psychology from the University of Wisconsin-Milwaukee, the Master of Divinity from Sioux Falls Seminary and the Doctor of Ministry degree from Palmer Seminary.

He has served pastorates in Kelowna, British Columbia and Ottawa, Ontario.

He joined the faculty of Briercrest College and Seminary in 1995 and has served there in full-time and adjunct capacities until the present.

He is a Clinical Fellow and Approved Supervisor with the American Association for Marriage and Family Therapy and a Registered Marriage and Family Therapist with the Canadian Association for Marriage and Family Therapy. He is also a Certified Professional Counsellor Supervisor with the Professional Association of Christian Counsellors and Psychotherapists.

He resides in Regina, Saskatchewan with his wife Erika.